RACE
TO THE
BOTTOM

RACE
TO THE
BOTTOM

CORPORATE SCHOOL REFORM AND
THE FUTURE OF PUBLIC EDUCATION

Michael V. McGill

TEACHERS COLLEGE PRESS

TEACHERS COLLEGE | COLUMBIA UNIVERSITY

NEW YORK AND LONDON

Published by Teachers College Press, 1234 Amsterdam Avenue, New York, NY
10027

Library of Congress Cataloging-in-Publication Data

McGill, Michael V.
  Race to the bottom : corporate school reform and the future of public
education / Michael V. McGill.
       pages cm
  Includes bibliographical references and index.
  ISBN 978-0-8077-5637-9 (pbk. : alk. paper) —
  ISBN 978-0-8077-7370-3 (ebook)
     1. Educational change—United States. 2. Education—Standards—United
States. 3. Public schools—United States. 4. Charter schools—United States. 5.
Privatization in education—United States. 6. Business and education—United
States. I. Title.
  LA217.2.M398 2015
  371.010973—dc23   2014046805

ISBN 978-0-8077-5637-9 (paper)
ISBN 978-0-8077-7370-3 (ebook)

Printed on acid-free paper
Manufactured in the United States of America

22 21 20 19 18 17 16 15   8 7 6 5 4 3 2 1

To Pucci, Wendy, David, and Erin for their belief and support, as well as to the dedicated educators, caring parents, and all the children I've been privileged to work with over the course of 5 decades

CONTENTS

CHAPTER 1

THE STATE OF EDUCATION

For nearly 3 decades, a powerful coalition of corporate leaders, politicians, and officials has engaged in a campaign to save the nation's "foundering" public schools. The stated goal of this crusade is to enable the United States to meet the economic challenges of the 2000s.

The strategy, sometimes called "corporate reform," is to take the methods that make businesses successful and apply them to schools, a prescription that is promoting mediocre education more appropriate for the 1950s than the 21st century. How did the country that invented the modern public school come to embrace policies that weaken it? What are the alternatives? How can we give America's children an education that will truly prepare them and our nation for tomorrow?

CORPORATE REFORM

The corporate reform agenda is simple: Impose rigorous standards. Demand accountability. Create competition. Accept no excuses. The plan is to use high-stakes exams to produce test scores, which become the main measure of an education. The data also become raw material for "analytics," which teachers and principals employ to address instructional shortcomings. Staff who don't meet performance targets are punished; presumably, punishment and competition will spur underperformers to improve or make them disappear.

To say that these ideas originate in the corporate world or that they reflect its pervasive influence isn't to imply that everyone in the private sector endorses them uncritically. Many Americans recognize that parallels between education and business ought to be treated gingerly. Still, the visceral appeal of the approach is strong, its advocates well organized and purposeful.

Critics of the movement have been unable to marshal nearly as compelling a narrative. Complexity is harder to understand than sound bites, and public education is nothing if not vast, varied, and complex.

In addition, the corporate reformers and a largely compliant press have deftly marginalized dissenters, portraying them as recalcitrant whiners who are the problem.

I have a different view.

My father was an educator, and I went into the family business. When I was 26, I became the director of a compensatory education program in New Hampshire. That was my introduction to what became a 40-year career in school leadership, the past 16 as superintendent in Scarsdale, New York. Along the way, education became my life. I found the work increasingly compelling, and I discovered that I was passionate about doing it well. That's my perspective, as I describe how the issues look and feel on the ground.

To begin: Although the teachers and school leaders I have encountered have had their share of flaws, most have been intelligent, positively motivated, and genuinely committed to children. The corporate narrative almost categorically fails to respect this resource. It wastefully disregards historical memory. Its self-certainty reflects disdain for public schools, as well as for the accumulated wisdom of the people who know them from the inside out.

An alternative to the corporate narrative might start with an observation by one of the nation's most distinguished education researchers, the late Seymour Sarason of Yale University. Considering the challenges public schools face, he said, it is astonishing they're as good as they are (1990, p. 8). Analysts as varied as David Berliner, professor emeritus at Arizona State University and former American Education Research Association president (Berliner & Biddle, 1995; Berliner, Glass, & Associates, 2007; Berliner & Nichols, 2014); Richard Rothstein of the Education Policy Institute (1998, 2008); and former U.S. assistant secretary of education Diane Ravitch (2010, 2013) have reinforced the point.

In the 20th century, public schools Americanized successive immigrant groups, responded to radical cultural changes and rising expectations, served a growing portion of an ever-more diverse population, and provided millions of people a ladder to better lives. Since the 1950s, ever-larger percentages of students have graduated from high school, and a growing portion has continued to postsecondary education (Bracey, 2002). According to the National Assessment of Educational Progress (NAEP), today's minority students are better educated than their White counterparts of the 1970s and substantially better educated than their predecessors ever were (National Center for Education Statistics [NCES], 2013).

So public education has much to be proud of. At the same time, it surely can be better. A fair assessment of the situation depends on a sense of context, however. For example, it's important to recognize that while individual teachers' strengths and weaknesses determine the quality of instruction in each classroom, the unevenness of teaching quality generally is more a result of the imperfect state of the art and of longstanding economic and social conditions. Beneath such evident difficulties lie less obvious philosophical and practical tensions that nobody has ever been able to resolve.

To complicate matters, the goal line keeps moving. Today's schools aren't just trying to educate more children to a higher level than ever before. They have to cope with unprecedented student diversity and the fallout from myriad social problems. They also struggle with mounting legal requirements and rising public expectations.

The corporate narrative largely avoids messy realities like these. One of its core assumptions is that past reforms failed simply because their authors got mired in detail or weren't persistent enough. To be more successful, presumably, change agents just have to be more strategic and efficient. They must do the following:

- Focus energy and resources on achieving numerical outcomes, demanding accountability, and creating competition
- Not let the education establishment whine, point fingers, or blame its failures on external conditions like poverty
- Stick unflinchingly to this strategy

After almost 3 decades of concerted effort, however, the results of these efficiency reforms have been unimpressive, especially if the goal is to provide an education that is excellent. Modest gains on national standardized tests have been far from commensurate with the effort expended and have not been markedly different from the growth that occurred in the 1970s and early 1980s. Meanwhile, test prepping is widespread and curriculums are narrower, shallower, and less engaging. Should young people study emerging social or political issues? Should teachers explore students' interests or teach what they love? Not on the syllabus.

Test-centric curriculums and budget slashing have caused many school districts to curtail or eliminate "nonessentials" like art, music, physical education, and world languages. Far too many educators feel disempowered and demoralized. Fearing punishment and undisposed to open rebellion, they submit to requirements that make little sense to them, comply with regulations that reduce them to objects, and do their best to breathe life into an education that increasingly seems inert.

At the same time, more than 4,700 charter schools now constitute over 5% of the nation's schools, serving more than 1.4 million students across the country (NCES, 2011). Free from bureaucratic fetters, these new institutions siphon resources from existing ones. Unlike schools in the regular system, they can dismiss students with behavior or learning problems. Many have added private funding. Nonetheless, they perform no better on average than their counterparts in the standard system, according to major studies.

ALTERNATIVES TO CORPORATE REFORM

Ironically, meanwhile, high-performing nations like Singapore and Finland have been trying to de-emphasize testing and accountability. But it shouldn't be surprising that America has headed in the opposite direction. Free-market values, including quantification, competition, and profit motive, are so ingrained in our culture that they almost inevitably have become favored approaches to what's called "the school problem"—as if all public schools really shared a single set of concerns.

It is not as if alternatives are lacking. America could have tried to improve the quality of its teacher talent pool or to address the effects of poverty on children's education. School accounts for only a limited part—perhaps as little as 20%—of what young people learn, and the link between parents' income and school success is well established (Goldhaber, 2002). Clearly, children are more apt to struggle when they come to school hungry or sick, when their family lives are unsettled, or when they are fearful for their safety outside of school.

Advocates for corporate-style change deflect such observations. "I know of no education reformer who talks solely of markets and ignores the critical interplay of challenging academic work and relationships between teachers and students," says Tennessee Education Commissioner Kevin Huffman (2014), for example. "And the idea that standardized tests are now the sole measure of success is laughable—in fact, qualitative observations of classroom instruction and interactions are the largest component of virtually every state's teacher evaluation system."

It is true that those who want to apply marketplace principles to education can also support other kinds of reforms. Nonetheless, the relentless focus on metrics, accountability, and competition has drained time, energy, and money from more crucial efforts to improve teaching and learning. Further, it has actively undermined educational quality. It has also diverted attention from broader issues—whether current levels of funding are adequate to make public education significantly stronger, for instance.

Imagine what might have happened, for example, if salaries had been high enough to attract the most able college graduates to teach in the first place and then to keep them from leaving for less frustrating and more lucrative jobs later. Or if we had offered robust support for teachers' and principals' ongoing education and development. No state and few communities have ever made that kind of commitment. Few are likely to do so any time in the foreseeable future.

In fact, the idea of improving teacher pay substantially or even of investing more in education generally would be almost unthinkable for many Americans. The concept is countercultural. Large numbers of taxpayers believe they are already spending about as much as they can afford on public services, even though the United States is less heavily taxed than all but three other countries (Korea, Turkey, and Mexico) in the Organization for Economic Community Development (Rampell, 2009).

To be sure, people in the United States do invest more in their schools than those in many other nations. Comparisons can be tricky, however. In the United States, for instance, school districts typically pay for employee health care; elsewhere, the nation may. Demographic and economic variables and scale also make a difference. Because of the large gap between rich and poor in America, our schools have a heavier lift than those in many other first-world nations.

Regardless, many Americans believe that it makes no sense to spend more on schools than they already do. After all, more money doesn't translate directly into better results, at least as measured by test scores. Why spend more, they ask, when we should get better value for what we already invest? Why pay teachers more when some of them are no good? There are many reasons not to do what self-evidently would improve education.

Therefore, the federal government and the states continue to emphasize accountability (testing, school competition, merit pay, and efforts to get rid of weak teachers and principals) instead of other reforms. How much will changes in tenure laws improve teaching if most performance problems are less about laziness or negligence and more a result of inadequate knowledge, time, or resources? How much testing is really necessary to monitor student growth and help teachers help their students?

Instead of exploring questions like these, the corporate reform strategy is to focus on a familiar array of bogeymen: lazy teachers, self-protective administrators, obstructionist unions. Nobody denies that these can be problems, but others are more fundamental and more serious. Some are amazingly obvious. It's hard for a teacher to make significant progress with students, for example, when a third of them enter and leave her class between September and December.

Unhappily, furthermore, advocates for the corporate strategy don't seem to be any less invested in their own version of reality as time passes.

President Obama (2011) may say that America's students "don't just memorize equations, but answer questions like 'What do you think of that idea? What would you change about the world? What do you want to be when you grow up?'" In the real world, however—the one I inhabit—federal and state policies push teachers and children to ask questions like, "Is A, B, or C the answer to number 15?" When parents—even parents in high-performance schools—get a principal's letter saying the regular program will stop in January so teachers can prepare children for state tests in the spring (a real story from a nearby suburban district), we're all in trouble.

Undaunted, corporate reforms pursue what organizational theorists call a "Theory X" approach to management: You control what you can't trust to work on its own. Specifically, Theory X assumes that the nation's educators do not have the knowledge, judgment, motivation, or skill to educate children well and won't in the foreseeable future. Therefore, they have to be regulated and compelled to do their jobs.

Is this the best America can do?

WHY "THE SCARSDALES" MATTER

I'm going to explore that question from a perspective that some people might describe as irrelevant. One of 700-plus school districts in New York State, Scarsdale is also one of the 100 wealthiest communities in the country. SAT scores are higher than those at many selective independent schools. Essentially everyone graduates. More than 95% of each graduating class attends a 4-year college. Typically, between 60 and 65% of students are admitted to the nation's most selective colleges and universities.

Once upon a time, "everyone" knew Scarsdale had the best schools in the country, as Debbie Reynolds told Frank Sinatra in the 1955 movie, *The Tender Trap* (though some in other communities might have disagreed). The school district had been featured in *Life* magazine and was mentioned in books about educational excellence. As educators and governments took up the cause of equity in the 1960s, however, Scarsdale and similar places began to seem irrelevant in the greater scheme.

For justifiable reasons, federal and state policymakers came to concentrate on urban education and on the achievement gap between White and non-White students. Graduate schools of education like Harvard and Teachers College at Columbia made city schools a priority. So it was and is reasonable to ask why policymakers—or anyone else—should worry about schools that serve the golden youth of the upper middle class, people who presumably will do well in life, regardless.

One response is that hundreds of thousands of young people are being educated in communities that share Scarsdale's general profile. Many of them will become leaders in their communities and states, the nation, and the world. What they do tomorrow will depend in no small part on their education today. The extent of their capacities and their concern for the common good will have a significant impact on our collective future. It may sound hopelessly old-fashioned, but in the end we all rise or fall together.

A second response might begin with an obvious question: What could the Bronx or Scarsdale possibly have to say to each other? On one hand is the edgy city; on the other, its elitist neighbor: the gritty real-world counterpoised with the bubble that protects the entitled and self-satisfied. Wouldn't exchanges among them be condescending or defensive?

Not necessarily.

I have three young friends, each involved in urban schooling. One has taught in a large urban middle school and at Island Academy, the prison school at Riker's Island in Queens, New York. Another is an elementary school principal in Worcester, Massachusetts, a city with a mixed population and modest resources. The third is a policy analyst in Manhattan.

Each one deals with issues that may appear remote from those in an affluent suburb. Nonetheless, the cities—their schools and their children—are no more monoliths of failure than their suburban counterparts are models of perfection. People everywhere come in all conditions. And everyone loses when we overlook what we have in common.

When I was in graduate school, one of my teachers showed us a film about a teenage boy in heavily African American Roxbury, MA. He introduced it as a glimpse into a unique coming-of-age experience in a particular subculture. As the movie unfolded, however, what I mainly saw was my own complex relationship with my father. Our differences notwithstanding, people are people, with similar struggles and joys. And school, in the end, is about human beings.

Third, educators everywhere have useful things to say to one another, even though conversations within school walls (let alone over them) can be difficult. It is true that daily life and work are consuming. Schedules conflict. In addition, when dialogue finally does start, it can end abruptly: "That approach might work there, but it could never work here." Nonetheless, the important question is whether broader ideas or principles might have relevance in places that are superficially dissimilar. To illustrate the point, I'll share a story about a lecture I once heard.

In the late 1800s, medical researchers learned that tine testing could identify tuberculosis victims for early, successful treatment. Nonetheless, the procedure wasn't used widely until well into the next century. Why?

To start, many physicians and pharmaceutical companies resisted, some because they had a financial interest in existing therapies. But a deeper problem was the fact that the new approach ran counter to their education and experience. They didn't want to give up practices they thought were effective. They knew what they knew and didn't want to believe they were wrong.

More broadly still, the general population saw tuberculosis as a social stigma, similar to AIDS in its early days. Families hid the sick in their homes or sent them to sanatoriums or other places far away. They resisted tine testing because they saw it as a threat, something that could expose their shame to others.

Medical education and public health policies ultimately overcame the professionals' certain but incorrect knowledge, as well as widespread lay resistance. Nonetheless, several decades passed before values and opinion shifted enough for people to change their behavior. Only then did most accept a practice that could have saved lives for years.

What does this story have to do with schools? After I left the lecture, I had a better understanding of why people and institutions are so slow to change. I also had greater appreciation for the tenacity and patience required for meaningful change. And I saw that a lot of a good leader's job is to educate people who may not think they need educating. I thought differently about my work.

A final reason for believing a Scarsdale matters is that all schools, regardless of how advantaged or disadvantaged, have cause to be concerned about corporate-style reform. The approach promotes standardization, which normally tends to bring practices and performance at the bottom and the top closer together. Some would call that "convergence on the average"; others would describe it as the definition of mediocrity.

Perhaps the best that can be said about the strategy, therefore, is that it offers a kind of structure and system that might be better than what already exists in places that are having trouble. But even that is no certain bet. In general, the schools that struggle most are ones where children lack the life advantages associated with academic success: good health care and nutrition, stable home lives, parents who themselves have strong educations. For many of these youngsters, their teachers and principals have to be a primary source of academic support and motivation.

The kind of education corporate reform promotes—getting children to score well on particular tests, for instance—isn't the same as enabling them to learn transferable skills, helping them to understand important concepts, or enlarging their appreciation for why a subject works the way it does. A focus on standardized exams doesn't engage them with language-rich literature. It doesn't encourage curiosity or promote independent learning. It doesn't make learning engaging or inspiring or memorable.

In fact, many children find formal education puzzling and artificial to start with. As they move through the grades and as curriculum grows more complex, it easily comes to seem even less relevant and more baffling. Those who lack the necessary skills, understanding, *and* an interest in learning have less and less incentive to play the school game as they enter adolescence. That is a prescription for academic disaster as they become less compliant, and take more responsibility for themselves. It is certainly not a promising strategy for developing well-educated citizens.

THE CHALLENGE

People can't solve the problems confronting a Boeing or Microsoft, let alone the issues of an interdependent global community, by the numbers. To make a difference, they need to think incisively and flexibly, to persevere and to collaborate effectively. In the words of University of Cambridge professor Michael McIntyre, they must possess "unmeasurables such as curiosity, interest and enthusiasm, and personal room for creativity" (2002).

Teachers cultivate these qualities through minute-by-minute interactions, making thoughtful judgments about the next step each pupil must take to realize her or his promise. The coursing heart of a real education is not a forced march in pursuit of higher scores, but the personal encounter between teacher and student. It depends on adults who are able to negotiate delicate webs of human interaction. The work is organic, complicated, and often maddeningly slow, a fact that holds just as true for school systems as it does for individual classrooms.

Yale's Seymour Sarason (1990) studied public schools for years, spending time in classes and talking with countless teachers and principals. Late in his long career he observed that their collective resistance to change wasn't so much a reflection of mulishness, or a lack of imagination, or the result of conspiracy. Deep reform, he said, is a matter of "recognizing and trying to change power relationships in complicated, traditional institutions, which are among the most complex tasks human beings can undertake" (p. 7).

Instead of respecting that reality, corporate reform crashes heedlessly ahead, ignoring context and avoiding searching reflection. In the process, ironically, it ignores important lessons from the private sector. Warren Buffett (2010) once described the importance of giving different divisions sea room. "Most of our managers," he said, ". . . use the independence we grant them magnificently, rewarding our confidence. . . . We would rather suffer the visible costs of a few bad decisions than incur the many invisible costs of decisions that [are the result of] a stifling bureaucracy."

In brief, there is a place for metrics, accountability, and competition in education, but some of the most successful corporations also emphasize other principles:

- Grant independence where possible; look for places where it is especially merited.
- Attract and retain highly qualified employees; develop their knowledge and skills.
- Invest significantly in research, development, and innovation at the grassroots level.
- Strip away bureaucracy; encourage initiative and creativity.
- Depend on smart, seasoned judgment; use numbers but don't count beans.
- Anticipate significant problems; intervene in operations only as necessary.

For more than 2 decades, I have listened while important state officials explained the imperatives of a one-size-fits-all reform strategy that ignores these principles. The plan has been to impose the same increasingly intrusive regulations on everyone regardless of meaningful differences among districts, schools, and educators. An obsession with accountability has overshadowed investment in professional growth. Instead of encouraging innovation, federal and state policies have created incentives that reinforce traditional curriculums, while driving teachers to prepare students narrowly for tests.

I might feel marginally better about this perverse situation if I thought it served some greater good. After years of trying to work with state and federal officials, however, I have yet to understand how it does.

Early on, the rationale for the massive superstructure of accountability was that everyone had to be treated the same because it was only fair; later, because lawsuits would ensue if different schools or different children were treated differently. In response to the observation that the law treats objectively different situations differently all the time, the justifications took a new turn. The mounting hours of standardized testing and its other intrusions weren't really problems at all. Scarsdale students would get good scores, so what *was* the problem?

Still later, a top state official dismissed Scarsdale's concerns as those of "a boutique operation." Another told a group of superintendents and board members that everyone has to be treated exactly the same because it is impossible to tell who the high performers are unless they all take the same tests (although there are clear and far less invasive indicators of success, like college acceptance records).

In short, I learned that a locality's needs, perspective, and whatever wisdom it had were relevant only to the extent they furthered the corporate agenda. Objections to the agenda seemed to be equated with disloyalty. The obsession with scores rolled on. The state received and spent millions of federal dollars building a massive testing and data collection system. The cost to local school districts was and is also in the millions; with 4,700 students, Scarsdale's direct costs for testing, data collection, uploading, and processing are close to $1 million each year and rising. Including indirect costs, the total is double that. The resulting data (which we are supposed to "mine," to use State Education Department [SED] jargon) are at best marginally useful.

So in the end, what do the systems and the numbers have to do with fostering better teachers or learners? As I've tried to cope with the self-certainty of corporate reform, I've kept asking myself what special insight its advocates have. Many of them are important people in responsible jobs and, surely, they must know something I don't. I ask colleagues across the nation what I'm missing. They respond with baffled resignation and a sense of disenfranchisement that is unique in my nearly half-century of school experience.

Still, I wonder whether I've become just another aging lion who wakes up each day creaky, sore, and hopelessly caged in the past. I think about when I taught in Massachusetts, just a kid watching the cynical veterans who used to fill the back row at faculty meetings, reading their newspapers while the principal talked. If I ever got to be like that, I thought, I'd want someone to, please, put me down. So I ask my colleagues whether I'm being crotchety or whether the situation really is as bad as I think it is. "Actually," one of them said recently, "it's worse."

I want to give the corporate reformers the benefit of the doubt. I know that some are idealists who want good schools for all. Some are more zealous: missionaries who believe they are bringing light to darkness. Some are technical adepts, pitching a sale with slick assurance and dancing on air. Others are more cynical. There is political hay to harvest and plenty of money to be made supplying the schools with the tools of the trade. Some want to replace public education with a cheap, balkanized system of privatized schools.

Regardless of what motivates it, however, corporate reform policy does not reflect a deep understanding of schools. Too often, it seems to be the product of a self-constructed reality that admits no real discussion or dissent, not contemplating the possibility that mandates can procure compliance and that mass production may raise test scores but that neither will make mediocre learning excellent. Nor will mandates and mass production give tomorrow's citizens or workers the quality education they need to succeed and contribute in a rapidly changing global community.

It's time to stop and begin again.

Whatever their shortcomings, Scarsdale and districts like it strive to give tomorrow's citizens an excellent education. They do their best to bring students into contact with bright, vibrant teachers. At their best, the strongest schools infuse education with meaning and insight; they transform lives. And that's the kind of experience every American child deserves.

CHAPTER 2

A BRIEF HISTORY (1787–2000)

In 1787, Thomas Jefferson espoused what was then the radical idea of educating all children at public expense. Implicit in his vision was a fundamental tension: How could schools produce a well-educated citizenry when the general population's aptitudes and interests differed so widely?

DEMOCRACY, EQUITY, EXCELLENCE

Jefferson's answer was that most people had limited academic ability and needed only a basic, utilitarian preparation for citizenship and work. Therefore, all free, male citizens would attend school for 3 years to learn to read, write, and figure. Then they would go on to farm, to apprentice in a craft, or to perform other kinds of labor (Jefferson, 1787/1984).

A much smaller number had the intelligence and the interest to go further. Suited for "leisure and learning," this relative handful would be "raked from the rubbish" to pursue something similar to what today we would call a liberal education. Through the study of classics, history, and natural philosophy, they would realize their individual potential and become personally fulfilled.

What was education worth in Jefferson's time? Since most people would need only basic skills and modest formal knowledge, they could be schooled at little cost. Meanwhile, higher learning was largely a process of one person's delivering and another's remembering content, and it involved a small percentage of the population. As a result, the minority who stayed on after the elementary grades could learn relatively cheaply, too.

Schooling underwent major changes after Jefferson's death in 1826. But for almost 200 years, his basic assumptions continued to typify thinking about public education. Some people were able; some weren't. They could be trained up in studies appropriate to their aptitudes at modest cost.

By the mid-1800s, immigrants from overseas had begun to flood the nation's urban centers. Many were poor, had little formal education, and spoke limited or no English. Their children came to school with all the associated academic disadvantages. As new compulsory attendance laws went into effect, furthermore, more students stayed in school until they were 14 or older. Unsurprisingly, the average level of performance declined. Problems increased. Critics called for reform.

EDUCATION AS ECONOMIC GOOD, SCHOOL AS BUSINESS

Charles William Eliot became president of Harvard in 1869. He was concerned that the public schools were not preparing a workforce to meet the needs of the economy. He had traveled in Europe, where nations were adapting their education systems to meet the needs of changing economies and emerging technologies. Returning to America, he championed a new core curriculum that would lead to specialized academic and vocational tracks of study. These would ready people of different abilities for their varied roles as workers.

In 1893, Eliot and a "Committee of Ten" eminent educators issued a report that urged adoption of these ideas and that would help to define the public school curriculum for the next century (Cremin, 1988). Over the next 30 years, schools also responded pragmatically to the increasingly diverse student population they were coming to serve. As a result, the single secondary education of Jefferson's time became several different ones (academic, vocational, and, often, general).

In an earlier iteration of corporate reform, schools began to use "scientific management" methods to make "production" more efficient and effective. The "principal teacher" became a school principal, a modern administrator who would efficiently manage a large factory-like operation according to cost-effective business principles. By the 1920s, furthermore, educators were using "scientific" IQ tests for student placement.

Developed to determine who was fit to fill the trenches during the Great War, these measures were valid and reliable (they tested what they were supposed to test and got consistent results time after time), although they didn't necessarily evaluate what was meaningful. Neither did they assess many aspects of intelligence, and those who promoted them wrongly assumed that intelligence was immutable (Lemann, 1999). Nonetheless, school administrators used them to decide which pupils were fit for vocational training, which should be elevated to academic classes, and which should drop out and go to work.

Popular beliefs about the effectiveness of business methods and the "science" of management continued to shape schooling for the next century. If these ideas had been less influential, ironically, we might be worrying less about educational failure today. Schools might have remained small and more personal. Tracking might not have existed, at least in its more pernicious forms. Well-educated teachers might have had time to find the talent that shone in every child. That wasn't what happened.

To summarize: For more than 100 years, public schools had operated on the assumption that education served two distinct purposes. It was valuable primarily because it was useful, a civic and an economic good. It was also a luxury: a source of personal enlightenment. The system further assumed that each individual had a fixed amount of ability. The first kind of learning was right for most people. A smaller number were more able and could benefit from an advanced education.

For all that time, also, the economy had depended primarily on workers' physical labor and practical intelligence. "Equal education" meant that everyone had an equal *opportunity* to learn ("everyone" being defined as White males). Most Americans assumed that the school's job was to put children on the same playing field and then let each one do what he could. Nobody expected every child to achieve at a high or equal level.

By assigning youngsters to different educations, the system closed off options and consigned people to lives of unrealized potential. Nonetheless, it seemed to work reasonably well for most Americans most of the time. Despite racial segregation, gender discrimination, the Depression and two world wars, enough people were educated well enough to meet workforce needs. And the simple fact of universal educational opportunity made the country a wonder of the world.

EDUCATIONAL REFORMATION: DEWEY AND PROGRESSIVISM

Nonetheless, the philosopher, psychologist, and educator John Dewey envisioned something better. Writing in the late 1800s and early 1900s, he turned traditional assumptions on their heads. Although people have different aptitudes, he said, everyone could benefit from learning that was both practical and "liberal," a preparation for lives of leisure *and* labor. A single democratic education—not separate tracks—was the answer (Dewey, 1916).

Instruction should evolve from students' interests and readiness. Lessons should mimic real-world activities, and students would "learn by doing," not just from books. Teachers should understand each child's thinking and then match academic content to individual needs in the moment. Students rich and poor would learn to understand themselves and one another by rubbing shoulders. Each would reach his individual potential, and together they would constitute a self-renewing democracy.

Dewey's progressive theories were hard to understand and easy to misinterpret. Too few teachers had strong enough academic backgrounds or the professional skill to tailor significant content to each student's evolving interests and needs. "Real-world" activities and "learning by doing" easily turned into "doing things" that displaced meaningful intellectual activity. Child-centeredness devolved into unhealthy permissiveness (Ravitch, 1983).

Coincidentally, and felicitously for the purposes of this narrative, Scarsdale became a national model of progressive practice during the 1920s and early 1930s. Each high school student had an individual learning contract that included independent research and tutorials, as well as group instruction. Elementary school children developed basic skills, engaged in interdisciplinary studies, and learned about personal responsibility by operating a store and a school farm.

The high school plan turned out to be labor-intensive and difficult for teachers to manage, however. Its novelty and unwieldiness also made it controversial. Elementary school parents complained that children weren't learning the three Rs. The quality of handwriting was declining.

After several years of community unease, the Board of Education appointed a champion of "fundamentals" to be its new superintendent of schools. At the most progressive of the elementary schools, the nationally recognized principal, Claire Zyve, resigned. Coincidentally, Scarsdale High School reinvented itself as a public version of a college preparatory school, complete with "deans" instead of guidance counselors.

Nationwide, retrenchment occurred in many schools that had tried to use progressive approaches. However, most schools had never sought to import the new practices in the first place. Even at the progressive movement's zenith in the 1920s and 1930s, the majority of parents and teachers resisted it actively. On the whole, teaching methods changed relatively little; schools looked much as they had in the past.

World War II effectively sidetracked the progressive movement. Lost in the process were initiatives such as the Eight Year Study, in which 250 colleges suspended their normal admissions criteria to allow a select group of high schools to try out nontraditional approaches to teaching, learning, and assessment. Students from these programs performed as well academically in college as students from more traditional schools and better in aspects considered more valuable than grades. When the study ended in 1940, however, so did the experiment (Ritchie, 1972).

COUNTER-REFORMATION: HUTCHINS AND TRADITIONALISM

America sought normality after the war. Suburbs expanded. New schools opened at a pace that favored the adoption of more traditional and less expensive programs, teaching methods, and testing. Even though progressivism's influence had been limited, longtime critics like the University of Chicago's president, Robert Maynard Hutchins (1936, 1953), continued to excoriate it for fostering an education that was insubstantial and insignificant.

Hutchins tapped into popular concern about declining standards and poor student performance, sentiments that were fueled by books such as Arthur Bestor's *Educational Wastelands* (1953/1985) and the anti-progressive *Why Johnny Can't Read* (Flesch, 1955). Nonetheless, Hutchins's broader message—that all students should have what amounted to a rigorous liberal arts preparation—never gained widespread support, if only because the word "liberal" sounded like a political statement. As before, public education in the 1950s consisted of a pragmatic blend of approaches that had no single, consistent philosophical foundation.

New methods continued to pile atop older ones. The quality of schools and teaching varied widely (Cuban, 1993). Most people assumed that students with different abilities should be assigned to separate programs. In time, many schools created even more tracks within tracks, offering more "educations" than before. In 1955, the Advanced Placement program created a new super level for the best and brightest.

Still, public schools did seem briefly to have found a stable, workable solution to the challenges of educating a highly diverse population to meet the needs of a democracy and its economy. In the late 1950s and 1960s, however, three historic developments upset this balance.

REVOLUTION

The Civil Rights movement translated the goal of providing equal opportunity into an even more idealistic attempt to produce equal educational outcomes. International competition spurred efforts to raise standards, especially in math and the sciences. And finally, the cultural revolution promoted the ideal of education for personal liberation and enlightenment, as distinct from education for economic or civic utility.

Civil Rights

In 1954, the U.S. Supreme Court ruled that racially segregated schools were inherently unequal and therefore unconstitutional. The response, desegregation, was an effort to equalize educational opportunity. However, the attempt to put everyone on a level playing field became intertwined with efforts to equalize outcomes—to close the achievement gap, in today's language.

A growing number of political activists, policymakers, and educators challenged a status quo in which African American children significantly underperformed their White counterparts. Their depressed achievement had nothing to do with innate ability, the activists said; it was the inevitable outcome of racial bias, low expectations, and poor schooling. The solution would be to treat all students as if they could learn at a high level and to give them the resources they needed to succeed.

Two important studies influenced this conversation. In 1966, a research team headed by University of Chicago sociologist James S. Coleman found that far more than any other factor, children's economic background correlated with academic success. Two years later, Robert Rosenthal and Lenore Jacobson's *Pygmalion in the Classroom* (1968) illustrated that students were more likely to succeed when their teachers believed they were able.

Over the next 20 years, education policy would embrace *Pygmalion*. Meanwhile, Coleman's (Coleman et al., 1966) work would be marginalized. It was controversial because economic levels and race correlate in America, a coincidence that seemed to suggest that children's race was responsible for their depressed performance. It was also inconvenient for policymakers and others who (for a variety of reasons) wanted schools to be entirely accountable for student performance.

Global Competition

The Soviet Union launched the world's first artificial satellite, Sputnik, in 1958, an achievement that shocked the United States. Suddenly, there was talk of Russian missile strikes from orbiting platforms. America's "failure" in the space race was widely seen as a result of its having lost superiority in engineering and technology. The obvious culprit was an education system that had treacherously, if unwittingly, ceded dominance to the Russians.

As if it were rehearsing for how it would react to Japan's economic rise in the early 1980s, big business decried the state of the public schools. The press contrasted the rigors of Soviet education with academic lassitude in the United States. The federal government then intervened in public education for the first time. The National Defense Education Act of 1958 funded efforts to improve math and science teaching. Experts from business and universities were consulted. A new generation of math and science curriculums issued forth.

The Soviet "advantage" turned out to be largely about paranoia and political spin. America's "failing" children went on to produce and innovate their way to unprecedented national prosperity. So what were Sputnik's real lessons? That perceived threats define people's reality and drive their behavior. That frightened people look for simple answers and someone to blame. That in that event, government and business assert themselves. That the schools are easy targets. Similar forces had already converged at the turn of the 20th century. They would again at the turn of the 21st.

The Cultural Revolution

In the mid-1960s, progressivism came back into fashion. Reacting against what the author Charles Silberman (1970) famously called America's "grim, joyless, and oppressive" classrooms, educators sought to make learning more personally rewarding (p. 11). The neo-progressives promoted an education that would be more "relevant" and meaningful. The "open classroom," "individualized instruction," and "creativity" were in vogue.

In 1977, for example, Scarsdale introduced an alternative school (the A-School) that John Dewey might have applauded. At democratic school meetings, young and old argued out differences over grading practices, academic requirements, and human relationships. Students were involved in project-centered assignments and other work that was intended to connect with their personal experiences and to engage their interests.

These forces—the Civil Rights movement, global competition, and the cultural revolution—profoundly unsettled the world of schooling in the 1960s and 1970s. Offering multiple educations, newly influenced by progressive ideas, and attempting to provide a wider range of children with a variety of new services, schools were thrust back into the crosscurrents of conflicting beliefs and rising expectations. They struggled to respond with limited financial and human resources.

Still more demands kept piling on. In the early 1970s, special education laws required public schools to provide services for a whole new class of people, many of whom previously had been left out or pushed out. In the process, they also spawned a welter of highly prescriptive regulations that directed disproportionate funding to a small segment of the population on the assumption that disproportionate need merited disproportionate support.

The federal legislation called IDEA (Individuals with Disabilities Education Act) also reflected and promoted a shift in views of the relationship between family and school. Before, education had been seen as an opportunity; IDEA furthered the belief that people were entitled to the education they wanted and deserved. Schools added programs and services as the new law required, but too often support was wanting; the full federal funding that was supposed to support IDEA never materialized.

COUNTER-REVOLUTION

In Scarsdale, the A-School gained credibility and thrived. More generally, however, neo-progressivism fell prey to old progressivism's woes. The scene was unhappily reminiscent of the 1940s and early 1950s. Some teachers ably employed neo-progressive practices while others "did their thing," to use the language of the time, and little significant, or at least testable, learning occurred. Meanwhile, in classrooms just down the hall, teachers could be talking most of the time while students listened, filled in workbooks, or did other seatwork. Even in New York City, where union and district leaders had endorsed the "open classroom," an estimated three-quarters of classrooms remained traditional (Cuban, 1993, p. 176).

Although student performance was improving according to the National Assessment of Educational Progress (NCES, 2013), many Americans blamed neo-progressive innovation for the "fact" that high school graduates couldn't read, write, or do math in the 1970s and 1980s. In the midst of this widespread dismay, it was easy to look back nostalgically to a mythical golden time that presumably had existed before the current Age of Lead.

The impulse was understandable, but as we have seen, the gauzy recollections of bygone days were more than a little ironic. Public schools had never educated everyone to a high level, and they had never been expected to do what they were being asked to do in the last third of the 20th century. Their shortcomings were as apt to result from mind-numbing tradition as from misguided innovation: The "tried and true" was often why they were wanting in the first place.

Regardless, any number of critics faulted schools for wanting to teach the "why" of math or for developing a questioning attitude toward history.

Students should learn to read, write, and figure, and to know their facts. They should become good workers. Some teachers responded by reverting to (or feeling validated in continuing to use) traditional approaches that involved drill or rote memorization.

In high-performing districts like Scarsdale, counter-reform took a different course. It was less about going back to traditional methods that had never been abandoned and more about an unrelenting emphasis on "rigor." It was hard not to be in favor of rigor, a word that invoked images of high standards and hard work.

Just as progressive ideas had been poorly understood and distorted, however, so was this one. Ideally, it would have been about engaging important ideas and learning to think well. But for many people, the way you knew courses were rigorous was that teachers assigned harder material and gave more homework. Rigor was about students' laboring longer hours to get good grades to get to the right college and a high-paying job.

A NATION AT RISK AND THE RISE OF CORPORATE EDUCATION

Such was the unsettled state of public education as an economically battered, politically shaken, and globally challenged nation trudged through the last of the dispiriting 1970s. And by the early 1980s, concerns about America's international economic competitiveness were prompting even more widespread apprehension. Falling SAT scores seemed to confirm the view that the schools were failing.

From this bleak landscape arose *A Nation at Risk* (ANAR), the report commissioned by U.S. Secretary of Education Terrel Bell. "If an unfriendly foreign power had attempted to impose on America the mediocre educational performance that exists today, we might well have viewed it as an act of war," the report said (National Commission on Excellence in Education, 1983. p. 1). Connecting the dots between the country's economic woes and its failing schools, ANAR offered a grim picture of a country reeling on the edge of decline and social disorder, a specter that must not be allowed to materialize, it said.

The parallels between 1983 and 1893 were striking: fear about the economy; international comparisons; a committee; a call to arms. Six of the 18 national commission members were from universities and one from a major research organization; five were political officials or representatives of groups like the National School Boards Association. Two were from private foundations. Four were public school educators, their minor role saying volumes about their perceived importance (National Commission on Excellence in Education, 1983).

Significantly, none of the commission members was a corporate leader. In this respect, ANAR not only ushered in a new era; it also represented an older one in which educators were viewed as stewards of their profession and public schools were valued for their civic role. As economic concerns came even more to the fore and the narrative of professional incompetence took hold, the business community would become far more visible in the school reform universe, where it would exercise significant influence.

Aiming to capture public attention, the report's rhetoric was purposely dramatic. Its actual agenda was more measured, calling for change along largely traditional lines: higher standards, better curriculums, more time in school, and stronger teaching. To re-read it today is to be struck by the way its relatively modest proposals contrast with the far more radical course that reforms took after 1983. At the time, however, it galvanized popular disappointment and frustration. For the most part, its assumptions and recommendations were accepted uncritically, and it quickly came as close as education news ever does to being a household commonplace.

ANAR's rapid popular acceptance may seem puzzling, particularly since many of its shortcomings were evident when it was published. The private sector's difficulties reflected the nature of an increasingly globalized economy as well as its own short-term, quarterly focus. Workers' difficulties often had less to do with their writing or math deficiencies than with the impossibility of anticipating and adjusting to rapid changes in the job market. SAT score declines largely reflected the fact that far more students were taking the tests, so that average scores were lower.

There was truth in the report, however. While schools in more affluent areas often offered a sound, and sometimes excellent, education, low expectations and substandard conditions were all too common, especially in lower-income communities. To be certain, this variability shouldn't have been surprising in a system comprising thousands of schools and hundreds of thousands of semi-independent teachers and administrators, especially given the nation's checkered education history.

Previous reforms hadn't changed the system. Still, some had shown promise, and some had made a real difference. For example, Linda Darling-Hammond (2001), nationally recognized professor of education at Stanford University, has argued that federal antipoverty education programs like Project Head Start narrowed the achievement gap between Blacks and Whites in the early 1970s. If the Reagan administration and its successors hadn't undercut those reforms, she says, the gap might not exist today.

While public education was far from perfect, therefore, many of its most serious difficulties reflected forces outside school walls. Others reflected informal contracts that local schools and their communities had worked out over generations—the exaltation of football teams over academics, for example. The situation merited a more generous and measured response than the one *A Nation at Risk* elicited. So how to explain the sense of betrayal it tapped, the anger it unleashed, and the "solutions" it generated?

For more than 2 decades, schools had struggled to adapt to rapid changes in demographics and social mores, as well as in family and student behavior. The adaptations often had less to do with teaching approaches or learning than with dress, speech, and other behavior that adults found unfamiliar or threatening. Parents sent their children to school to be cared for and protected; the schools were supposed to stay safely, predictably the same, as they had been in a recollected, sometimes imaginary, past. They easily could seem to have betrayed this trust.

Furthermore, instead of being grateful recipients of educational opportunity, more citizens were likely to see themselves as consumers who were entitled to buy what they wanted at the education store. The storekeepers inevitably disappointed customers. The education establishment also had less control over consumer dissatisfaction. In small-town America, they had relied on residents' interdependence and on personal relationships to control and mediate conflicts. Especially after the social and political transformations of the 1960s, dissatisfaction in a more urbanized America was more likely to erupt publicly.

At the same time, the schools were politically vulnerable, easy targets for populists, politicians, and opportunists who had their own agendas and little interest in education's complexity or in addressing the social, political, or economic roots of the system's problems. They did have bully pulpits, which they used. These forces also fed public disillusionment.

But the business community's involvement was critical. Corporate and political leaders had come to believe that education really did matter to the economy and (therefore) to them. Company presidents and governors worried about the challenges of international business competition. Especially in the New South, politicians feared for their states' economic viability. A better educated workforce seemed essential to the economy and the national interest.

Cheered on by newspaper editorial pages, new business and government coalitions announced plans to reform all or parts of America's vast, loosely connected state networks of schools. They would take the management methods that had made the private sector such a success and apply them to public education—a strategy not without its ironies, considering the harvest of economic problems that lay in the future. In the late 1980s, states like Arkansas and Tennessee decided to force schools to improve by tightly controlling production and output standards, and by holding employees accountable for the results—in theory, at least, just as business did.

ESCAPING HISTORY

By 1994, these initiatives had come together through the efforts of a national coalition that persuaded Congress to approve a bill called "Education Goals 2000." Supported by the Clinton White House, the legislation set the objective of making all students in grades 4, 8, and 12 "proficient" in the major academic subjects by the turn of the new century. Ninety percent would graduate from high school. The United States would be first in the world in science and math.

A year later, therefore, New York State's education governors, the Board of Regents, were squarely in the national school reform mainstream when they decided to escape history. In order to graduate, every student in each of the state's 754 school districts would have to earn a Regents' diploma, signifying that he or she had completed what historically had been a college preparatory program.

At the urging of Education Commissioner and corporate reformer Richard Mills, the Board of Regents mandated new tests to monitor the progress of each student in grades 3 through 8; they then required everyone to pursue a high school curriculum originally intended for the college-bound. Every youngster would have to pass the same seven high school exams to graduate. Schools and administrators would be punished for failing to meet the scoring targets that marked success.

The goal was noble, the hubris of trying to achieve it quickly, by fiat, strangely impressive. Notionally, at least, the Regents had resolved in a single bold stroke the ancient Jeffersonian tension between equity and excellence, something no one had been able to do for 200 years. Every student in New York State, regardless of background, aptitude, or interest, would have an equal education *and* meet a single high standard of learning.

What the initiative didn't do was at least as telling as what it did. First, it set a higher and perhaps unreachable bar without adding enough resources to enable the schools to reach it. The state failed to comply with a court decision that low-wealth districts should receive more funding. State aid increases would keep pace with normal enrollment growth, rising special education costs, and other requirements.

Second, instead of understanding the story of public education as a tale of hard-won, if partial, gains in the face of ever-growing demands and longer odds, the plan invoked a familiar narrative of failure. The fault for children's struggles lay entirely with the schools. Poverty, social conditions, and other external factors were irrelevant. Instead of helping teachers and administrators do a better job, the strategy was to punish them for failing.

And as they tried to step out of history, the Commissioner and Regents also ignored some of its most important lessons: Efforts to transport business methods into schools were responsible for many of the current woes of public education in the first place. Global economic competition was a concern, but America's resilient public schools were a resource that had educated generations of innovative, productive citizens. Education in a democracy has purposes other than job preparation.

It would have been wiser to innovate with a sense of humility. It would have been intelligent to build on the strengths of a system that had contributed so significantly to the nation's past success. It would have been far-sighted to treasure institutions that were in a unique position to realize the nation's civic and social ends. It still would be, today.

CHAPTER 3

TEST WARS AND THE
EMPIRE STRIKES BACK (2001)

By the late 1990s, corporate reform had begun to evince a sort of karmic inevitability. Business leaders, politicians, and journalists, as well as many ordinary citizens, believed it was about time the failing schools finally shaped up. And given its provenance, Scarsdale was an unlikely seedbed of resistance.

UNLIKELY REBELS

At the center of downtown Scarsdale stood a massive Tudor-style business-and-office building of brick and half-timber, a towered symbol of material aspiration and achievement. Designed to evoke an imagined English past, this monument to retail and the professions had displaced a more modest and eclectic American main street in the early 1900s.

Outside the center was a landscape of what a 1920s brochure described as "fine country estates." By the 1990s, it had come to consist of elegant turn-of-the-century residences and comfortable homes built later, as well as more recent "McMansions." Green spaces laced through the community; the longstanding metaphor for the place was "a village in a park."

Over the years, Scarsdale had become a cultural touchstone, a symbol of the American dream in the favored suburbs. Emblematic was one in a long line of similar *New Yorker* cartoons: A rumpled guitar player sits at a microphone in Greenwich Village. "This next one is a blues about hard times," he says, "and the 5:06 being late to Scarsdale."

Stereotypes notwithstanding, the community was home to a sizeable international and minority population. Its style was generally traditional, and change could be achingly slow; it took over a decade to begin to replace a bridge over the railroad tracks. Residents valued civic activity and volunteered for roles in local government. They created an early childhood center, a family counseling service, and other social outreach programs. Youth leagues were a big deal.

Decency and venality, fallibility and generosity seemed to be distributed in the usual proportions. The inevitable complaints about incivility and entitlement had to be understood in context. At a meeting in my previous district, an angry young mother had stood up and told me that my failure to get a stop sign installed on a public street (not actually part of a superintendent's job description) was going to cause her child's blood to be on my hands. In Scarsdale, for the most part, people supported the community, the schools, and one another. At moments of tragedy or crisis, they could be magnificent.

In fact, most adults and youth were thoughtful and articulate, and they displayed a variety of styles and almost every viewpoint you could imagine. The well of talent ran deep. Some of the most accomplished and most privileged were the most human and down to earth. Parents seemed to employ a normal range of approaches to childrearing, although the young often did appear to enjoy an especially sunny place in the family circle.

From time to time, unhappy events occurred. Adults did regrettable things, and teenagers got in trouble. Although human frailty is everywhere, outsiders often seemed to think its existence in Scarsdale said something special about the place. Kids came to a dance under the influence, and like *Casablanca's* Inspector Renault, the New York papers and the regional TV station were positively *shocked*. After another bad weekend, a regional newspaper blog read, "I hear some Scarsdale kids got into a fight at a party." "No way," was the reply. "What did they do, throw pennies at each other?"

The stereotypes were unfair to people who were more individual, interesting, and human—more normal—than whatever the image might have been. Still, some generalizations were legitimate. Scarsdale understood competition and achievement. Education was and is a priority.

The business of the district has always been to prepare every student for success in college, and the results speak for themselves. Residents tax themselves heavily to support the schools. Still, whatever the impression elsewhere, not everyone is unremittingly wealthy, and some parents sacrifice significantly to give their children a Scarsdale education.

Just as important, the parents are part of an ongoing and self-reinforcing cycle of achievement, motivation, and investment. Unlike communities where arguments over funding or other priorities set teachers, parents, and other residents against one another, Scarsdale historically has attracted new generations of homeowners who feel a sense of ownership for the schools.

SCARSDALE AND STATE TESTING

Under the circumstances, one might have expected residents to place a premium on top test scores. But until the State Education Department (SED) introduced its new test regime in 1995, state exams hadn't been a significant concern. Essentially, the schools and community had concurred quietly that the tests that really mattered were college admission and success in life.

Some would have said that this attitude was evidence of arrogance and elitism. Others would have recalled that the district had taken an independent approach to education for almost a century. That wasn't the case in 1996, however. Although the district's elementary schools had been among New York's highest scorers on the state's new tests, two of the schools had ranked below the other three. Principals and teachers painfully found, from phone calls and heated comments at meetings, that second best was not okay.

Unsurprisingly, faculty members had concluded that students had better get top scores. To question that premise or the tests' validity was seen as politically suicidal. The faculty organization president told her constituents to say they supported the state's new testing regime. Thereafter, they'd have two somewhat contradictory objectives: to make sure scores were high and to keep test preparation from becoming an obsession.

When I was appointed Scarsdale's ninth superintendent of schools in 1998, I had already been critical of what I saw as the state's inordinate emphasis on testing. I had said it would intrude on local autonomy, displace valuable learning, and get in the way of teaching important material that wasn't tested. And it wouldn't add useful information to what many districts already knew from other assessments.

If accountability was the issue, Scarsdale could share graduation and college admissions data, SAT scores, and Advanced Placement results. Over 90% of special-needs students attended college, and their SAT scores were higher than the regular national average. We could develop added measures that actually would help us to improve our work: invite external panels of educators to validate the quality of our programs, for instance.

THE COSTS OF STATE TESTS

By the fall of 2000, Albany had announced plans to expand its 8th-grade tests from the original two (math and English) to five in five different subjects. Teachers would have to sit through orientation sessions. Students would take the tests. The teachers would correct them. In science alone, this activity would displace 9½ days of instruction for each student. Administering and correcting the full battery of exams would consume a minimum of 22 days out of a 180-day year for every student, not counting added test prep. While teachers corrected the tests, the school would have to hire substitutes. That would cost a quarter of the annual substitute teacher budget.

Scarsdale's middle school principal, Michael McDermott, wasn't happy. Since the new science test would cover 4 years, students would have to review material they had studied as far back as 5th grade. How many people remember material they learned 4 years ago well enough to answer questions on a multiple-choice test? Review sessions necessarily would reduce the time for studying new material. Some existing curriculums would have to go.

Eighth-graders studied Gulf Coast storms on computers in real time. The content was timely and interesting, and kids usually got excited about the science. They used mathematical models to simulate weather patterns and graphed the progress of actual systems. But teachers could cover the unit on weather faster if they dropped the online experience. The hurricane study would be sacrificed.

Students also used computer software instead of old triple beam balances in lab experiments. But triple beam balances were still standard issue in many New York schools, and they might be on the state test. Would the school buy triple beam balances and teach students how to use them, or would it risk lower test scores?

The social studies department head spoke passionately about the drawbacks of studying history as if students were in a car headed down an expressway toward a May test rendezvous. History should be a canoe journey down a river, he said, where you could take unexpected turns and stop to explore. But now, teachers would curtail or avoid altogether the several-day exploration of women's roles in Colonial America, even if students really wanted to know more about the subject. There would just be less time to make connections that illustrated why history is relevant to events today.

There wouldn't be time to study the Elizabethans in social studies or perhaps even to mount scenes from Shakespeare in English; the Elizabethans wouldn't be on the test. The English department was stressing literature less anyway; teachers needed to spend more time on students' listening and speaking. Who could be against that, even if the new curriculum would be less academic?

The mathematicians were pragmatists. To cover everything that might be tested, they would have to skim over some topics, teach in less depth, and spend less class time on students' interests or on their questions. "Parents haven't complained very much," the department chair said. "We'll do our best with what we've got. The program just won't be what it was."

The losses might have been less troubling if the tests had yielded valuable information about children's strengths and weaknesses. But teachers across the state corrected the tests in marathon sessions that were controlled for security. In Albany, officials reviewed them and decided what the "passing" score would be. Papers then got ranked in categories from the desirable Level 4 down to the dread Level 1. When the results came back to the schools months later, there was no way to tell which questions any individual student had gotten right or wrong.

Individual scores weren't available, but group scores were. Sometimes, that information might help teachers understand which topics needed more emphasis; sometimes there was no way to know why children had gotten answers either right or wrong or what to do about it. Even if the results had been more useful, they were less powerful, less discriminating duplicates of other measures the school already used. In fact, state exams in previous years hadn't turned up a single at-risk student who hadn't already been identified by teacher observation, class grades, or other standardized tests that were built specifically for high-performing public and independent schools.

Usually, state officials, business leaders, and newspapers could characterize dissenters like McDermott as defensive, grumpy hand-wringers. But Scarsdale students were among the top performers in the state, so it was hard to call him a whiner. Still, he and other Scarsdale people *could* be characterized as elitists who thought they shouldn't be held to the same standards as everyone else. And that turned out to be a main line of attack.

CIVIL DISOBEDIENCE

If the rationale for the state plan had been more convincing or if the plan had been more limited, parents might not have flirted with civil disobedience. But even a visiting state spokesman acknowledged that all of the exams didn't seem necessary, since the math and English scores correlated highly with science and social studies results. Just as unsettling, the existing 8th-grade tests didn't consistently predict high school performance, which is why the whole system was supposed to exist in the first place.

A Scarsdale civic association invited state Education Commissioner Mills and members of the Board of Regents to come and discuss the issues in February 2001. Several of the Regents and a lower-level State Education Department (SED) official appeared. Members of the state team proposed variously that tests would help Scarsdale; they wouldn't help Scarsdale, but were important elsewhere; and everyone in the state should be treated the same because "the same" was fair.

In March, the district Parent Teacher Council invited the author, lecturer, and neo-progressive education advocate Alfie Kohn to speak. A 1960s-style activist, Kohn offered a passionate, acid, and funny critique of standardized testing and of the state's testing system more specifically. By mid-month, a growing number of parents had begun to talk about boycotting the exams. A newly formed community group called STOP (State Testing Opposed by Parents) was organizing resistance and urging families to keep their children home on the days the tests would be given.

Neither the Scarsdale Board of Education nor school administrators had hidden their reservations about the tests. Nonetheless, they were legally bound to enforce state regulations. The district therefore took the position that students should come to school and take the exams. But what would happen if families kept their children home?

If the middle school followed its usual procedures, nothing. State test scores had never counted in children's grade averages there, so there was no academic penalty for absence. If a student missed both a state test and the test makeup, neither Albany nor the school required follow-up. And for several reasons, it seemed inappropriate to adopt new penalties now for students who didn't take the exams.

Normally, if a child was absent because of a parent's actions—if a family left for vacation early, for instance—the school didn't penalize the child. Instead, the principal or a counselor would talk with the parent and work out a way to avoid future difficulties. If a student didn't take one of the state tests because her parent told her not to, it seemed equally unjust to punish her for the parent's decision.

So if the school administered its rules as usual, there would be no immediate penalty for either children or their families. That increased the likelihood of a boycott. If that occurred, Albany officials, wanting resistance quashed and the issue to go away, would criticize and possibly punish Scarsdale.

If the school changed its rules, on the other hand, it would have to punish children for their parents' actions. Or it might press truancy charges against parents in court. But as the district's legal counsel said in one discussion, a judge would very probably throw the charges out.

And of course, even if the school did somehow force children to come into the building, teachers weren't going to force them to fill in the blanks if they didn't want to. Additionally, some parents already were beginning to talk about the boycott as a First Amendment issue. Whatever the district did, the community could be seriously divided.

Considering these possibilities, and acting on my recommendation, the Board of Education told the school to follow its normal procedures and stated its opposition to a boycott. The faculty were to stop test prepping, provide a deep, rich education, and let exam results take care of themselves. The district would use existing local, state, and national measures for accountability.

This policy statement would turn out to be the most important legacy of the spring of 2001. Although it proved impossible to discourage all test prepping, most teachers subsequently did seem to view the state exams with a measured perspective. As long as the quality of instruction remained high, students were learning, and college admissions remained strong, most parents seemed satisfied. In fact, it appeared that Scarsdale might be able to sustain what was, in the world of public education in 2001, a remarkably balanced approach to high-stakes testing.

As the test dates approached, *The New York Times* printed the first in what would turn out to be a series of stories, this one saying that Scarsdale administrators were offering their consent and even subtle advice to the test "rebels" (Zernicke, 2001). The next weeks slid into a blur of controversy, public relations, and interviews: NBC nightly and local news, National Public Radio, CNN, local Channel 12, *The New York Times*, *The Washington Post*.

The breaking story also incited inconclusive exchanges with Albany. Secondhand, district officials heard that SED was saying students should take makeup tests if they missed the regular ones. A Scarsdale trustee reported that one of the Regents had contacted her informally, saying that the state board had discussed ways to retaliate against the district for its independence: The Board of Education should immediately write *The Times*, disavow the boycott, and demonstrate that it would force students to take tests. The local board declined.

The future seemed decreasingly clear. If the state wanted to administer discipline, the apparent recourse would be to try to remove the board and/or the superintendent. Nobody knew where such an effort would lead because the only precedents involved cases of corruption or long-standing school failure. For the state to initiate a head-to-head fight with the trustees of one of the highest-performing public school districts in the nation would be a very different proposition. Displacing a governing board was difficult business even when schools were dysfunctional, and that was clearly not the case in Scarsdale. Furthermore, board members had the confidence of a highly educated, articulate, and politically powerful community. There would be no shortage of lawyers available to defend a First Amendment case.

In Scarsdale's view, there was little to be gained from an ongoing and increasingly personal conflict with the Commissioner and Regents. Going forward, the school district had to work with the state. It didn't need a confrontation or the associated publicity. Just managing the current regional and national media attention had already been a significant distraction from the work of educating students.

As far as the district's lawyers knew, the situation had no real parallel. If the case got to the courts, it could take years to resolve. Everyone faced the prospect of a long, twilight struggle with no clear victory. As the adults continued to worry about these kinds of political issues, the middle school prepared to give children the state tests. On the first day, 67% of 8th-graders were absent from the English exam. In social studies and science, absences would turn out to be as high as 70%.

SCARSDALE AND ALBANY

Albany authorities said the Commissioner might initiate an investigation. The head of the regional Board of Cooperative Educational Services, an arm of the State Department of Education, advised local board members "not to trust" the powers-that-be upstate. According to an official spokesperson, meanwhile, the Regents were satisfied that Scarsdale had followed appropriate procedures. At the same time, the Commissioner reportedly had told a roomful of people that he deemed the boycott "as serious as a case of cheating." And the newspaper *Newsday* quoted Regent Robert Johnson as saying it was "not happenstance" that the boycott happened where it did. "The superintendent has said he has not aided and abetted the parents. Others say he clearly has" (Goodman, 2001).

From the State Education Building in Albany, 110 miles to the north, the school district doubtless looked disloyal and disingenuous. What in Scarsdale seemed to be an honest expression of disagreement very probably seemed like a threat to be crushed, although SED publicly downplayed its importance.

The large number of students who stayed away from the tests indicated the sentiment of most parents. Less vocal residents were troubled by what they saw as a statement of exceptionalism: the idea that Scarsdale shouldn't follow the same requirements that applied to everyone else. Some people were just bothered by all the attention. Critics beyond the village borders said the boycott revealed the community's elitism.

A mother from a nearby district wrote the regional paper, for example, to say Scarsdale parents were afraid their kids wouldn't get good scores. They were selfish, trying to subvert tests that would benefit everyone else. Sympathizers, meanwhile, thanked Scarsdale for doing what they couldn't. They lived and died by the scores; if they expressed their concerns about testing publicly, they said, they'd be discredited and punished.

At a state teachers' union convention, a delegate who announced he was from Scarsdale reportedly received a standing ovation from 3,200 rank-and-file delegates, while Commissioner Mills looked on from the dais. Positions hardened. Feelings intensified. For the moment, at least, Scarsdale was on the front line of Test Wars.

Confronted by test rebels in an outlying sector of the galaxy, Commissioner Mills appointed an investigating team. It would ask three questions: Had the district followed state requirements for administering the tests? Had it followed its own procedures for handling absences? What were its plans to provide academic support for children who didn't take the tests?

The team arrived in late spring of 2001; looked mainly at procedures, handbooks, attendance rates, and other objective information; spoke with a handful of people; and left. Summer came, drifted on, and the long days slipped into autumn. In late October, a state official called to say the commissioner had written the school district a "measured" letter to bring matters to a close without further enflaming the situation.

The actual correspondence wasn't so benign. Criticizing the district for having abetted the boycott, it sought assurances there'd be no recurrence. Scarsdale had failed to "strictly adhere to its own local attendance policies," the letter charged. Not only that, the district had acted in bad faith; local educators had "repeatedly stressed" that "the State Assessments were irrelevant and purposeless." Furthermore, the district had invited boycott advocates to speak with parents but failed to present a countervailing point of view. Its actions "may have resulted in some students' failing to be identified for Academic Intervention Services" (Mills, 2001).

Local officials responded: First, the "misapplied" attendance policies the commissioner referred to were in a high school handbook. They had nothing to do with the middle school. Second, contrary to what the commissioner asserted, the middle school principal had said in a newsletter that he'd "always emphasized that the content of [state] assessments has educational value." The issue was one of "cost and benefit." Third, citizens, not the district, had sponsored the panel of state officials and the speaker Alfie Kohn, thereby addressing different sides of the test issue (McGill, 2001).

The one point of more serious concern was the charge that the district's actions could have prevented students who needed academic help from getting it. The assertion assumed that students' scores on the 8th-grade tests predicted their performance in high school. But did that correlation actually exist? One of the state panel speakers had told an auditorium full of Scarsdale residents that there was none.

Further, students who scored poorly on state tests had already been getting extra help. And in previous years, many who were less successful on their 8th-grade tests had gone on to do well in high school, while a number who had trouble in high school had succeeded on the exams. The empirical evidence did not support the idea that needy students would suffer.

In its response to Mills, the district affirmed that it would continue to abide by state law, regulation, and directives. Albany offered no further intelligence. As the weeks passed, and especially after September 11, 2001, the boycott seemed less and less consequential. Fewer families told their children not to take state tests in 2002. In 2003, over 95% of pupils were physically present, but about 15% checked a box indicating they refused to take the exams.

According to New York's interpretation of the federal No Child Left Behind law, Scarsdale Middle School had failed to meet minimum test attendance requirements. So in 2004, the school was declared "in need of improvement," along with more than 700 other New York public schools. (A scary figure if, indeed, that was close to an accurate estimate of a real problem.) If the situation continued, the school would have to submit a compliance plan in which it presumably would have to show how it would get parents to get their children to fill in answer blanks. More draconian penalties could follow.

Among parents, there seemed to be tacit consensus that they had done what they could do and that the schools had done their best to explain their case. Speaking personally, I'd directed huge amounts of energy to boycott-related contacts with the media, attorneys, parents, community, Albany, and the Board of Education. I was shortchanging important parts of my work. The board, other administrators, teachers, and parents also had been caught up in the whirlwind. It was time to focus on teaching and learning.

The district was never asked to supply a remediation plan; by 2006, the middle school was meeting its mandated attendance target.

REFLECTIONS ON A SMALL REBELLION

In the midst of the corporate-style crusade to transform public education, the worries in an affluent community didn't elicit much sympathy. There was some public interest in the mothers who'd organized the boycott, as well as some mockery of "soccer moms." At the very best, the public and the press seemed ambivalent about the story.

What version of the truth would prevail? There was never really any question. The boycott and its aftermath may have had little to do with educational equity in New York State and a lot to do with what made educational sense in Scarsdale. But neither the educational merits nor the facts really mattered. Not wanting to open the floodgates to resistance in other communities, state officials saw a political problem, which they managed deftly. Their objective was to control the public agenda. They used factually inaccurate information to justify problematic conclusions. They had power. They had access to the press.

If nothing else, Richard Mills was a man of steely authority. He held a position that commanded public respect. He was smart and articulate. Employing martial rhetoric about his "unflinching determination," he positioned himself as the defender of New York's children. Implicitly, elitist Scarsdale was selfish; parents and local officials were just for themselves and their children and against everyone else's.

State officials didn't have to say that; they had newspapers to discredit Scarsdale for them. Under the elegant headline "Scarsdale School Suckers," for example, *The New York Post's* Arnold Ahlert (2001) lambasted parents for objecting to tests "that stress objectivity over subjectivity" and blasted the "educrats" who'd duped them into believing that facts weren't important (although objections to the tests had nothing to do with either issue). Then, following September 11, 2001, a somewhat overwrought columnist in the regional *Journal News* connected the World Trade Center disaster and test skeptics, verging on the implication that they were somehow fellow travelers of Al Qaeda because they didn't want students to learn about global issues (also not true) (Nikolski, 2001).

On the Friday before the Commissioner's determinations were to be released, Deputy Commissioner James Kadamus contacted Scarsdale to say that the district would see the conclusions before they became public late the following week. Instead, Albany released its report to the press almost simultaneously; on Wednesday, *The New York Times* published "No More Test Boycotts, Scarsdale Is Warned" (Harticollis, 2001). Scarsdale had no time to read the report or to respond thoughtfully.

Then, after months in which reporters had inquired avidly about local responses to Albany's actions, *The Times* dropped its coverage. Had other events made the story insignificant? Had editors concluded that in the big picture, Albany was right, so the particulars didn't matter? Was it just time for the story to die? All in the category of "Things We'll Never Know."

For me, one of the most poignant lessons of the Spring 2001 test boycott appeared in the form of an email late in the fall. "As a NYC public school teacher who works at a middle school where 300 families apply for 100 seats, yet was deemed to 'need improvement . . . ,' I applaud your efforts up north," it read. "It's refreshing to see a place with common sense and an obvious respect for teachers, students, and the entire school community. Thanks for helping us fight the good fight."

Scarsdale could say things few others could or would. Many teachers and administrators believed that the testing wasn't helping them overcome the obstacles they faced every day, but they didn't say so. As a fellow superintendent said, "The train's left the station. Just move on." Since 2001, matters haven't changed that much.

CHAPTER 4

THE TRIUMPH OF CORPORATE REFORM (2001–2014)

In the early 1900s, "scientific management" methods espoused by the industrial engineering expert Frederick W. Taylor had reshaped public schooling. A half-century later, W. Edwards Deming's theory of Total Quality Management (TQM) was similarly influential. The approach grew out of efforts to help reconstruct Japan's manufacturing economy after World War II (Deming, 1986).

The idea was to set measurable performance targets ("So many widgets will meet the following specifications"), hold workers accountable for meeting them, and provide the workers with substantial latitude to figure out how to get there—a process of "controlling ends tightly" while "controlling means loosely." When metrics showed that the targets were being met, a company would adopt more ambitious ones in a process of "continuous improvement." The ideal (and unattainable) goal was a "zero defect" product.

As Japan's economic fortunes rose in the 1970s and 1980s, Deming became a sort of American business icon, and corporate leaders promoted the methods he had helped pioneer. Especially after *A Nation at Risk,* TQM and complementary approaches (like those espoused by the University of Toronto's Michael Fullan) began to spill over from business to education (Fullan, 1982, 1993, 2001). Among the first to advocate their use were corporate heads and governors from states like Arkansas, Tennessee, Florida, and Texas.

CONTENDING AGENDAS

The politicians came mostly from southern and mid-southern states with ailing agricultural and manufacturing sectors. In search of a brighter technological and industrial future, they sought to create a new economy, one that would require an educated workforce. Unfortunately, the general quality of education in their states was notoriously weak. Self-evidently, business-like efficiency and competition in the school "marketplace" would produce better results.

While some saw this emerging corporate and political consensus as a sinister conspiracy, it was more likely to reflect the sort of accepted wisdom that evolves through interactions in boardrooms, elite university seminars, "summit meetings," and social events. Some who espoused it were grasping or opportunistic, but many were sincerely trying to do the right thing.

Meanwhile, any number of educators believed that TQM and similar approaches might help public schools recover a clearer sense of direction. The institution was trying to serve a larger portion of the population than ever, and since the 1950s, it had taken on more and more responsibilities, from special education to drug education to sex education. As it struggled to achieve a wide range of objectives, it seemed to be doing nothing very well. TQM could help clarify its academic mission.

The approach also might help to resolve the inconclusive and polarizing struggle over educational ends and means that had preoccupied neo-progressives and back-to-basics advocates since the late 1960s. Teachers and schools would be able to use either more or less traditional methods, or both, as long as children learned what they were supposed to learn. What mattered was whether students got to the goal, not how the teacher got them there.

The difference in corporate and educators' perspectives was not confined to ideas about TQM. Any number of educators held that high standards were essential and that schools should improve continuously. They recognized that teachers can have an important impact on students. However, they also thought that schools were unlikely to achieve much better results as long as pernicious social and economic conditions went unaddressed.

The more simplistic corporate position seemed to be that schools should be able to get all students to achieve at a high level, period. They would learn if teachers and schools would stop blaming social conditions or children themselves for their failures and just do their jobs. It might be desirable to overcome economic and social inequities, but business, government, and the society at large need not address them in order to solve the nation's education problems.

Educators and corporate reformers also had different explanations for why public schools hadn't improved the general level of learning more than they had. In the corporate view, large numbers of educators were self-serving, lazy, or worse. The solution was to hold them accountable through the business-like use of goals, metrics, and accountability.

Punishment would force them to get children to meet predetermined numerical benchmarks.

Educators would admit that obstinate teachers, unions, and other corporate reform shibboleths could be problems. But they also thought the more fundamental difficulty was that teachers often lacked the knowledge to achieve better results than they did. Frequently, the knowledge didn't even exist and nobody knew what the solutions might be. In this view, a stronger talent pool, better professional education, and more research were essential.

There were also different views of the value of metrics and technology. Corporate America had honed the use of metrics to a fine edge and made statistical analysis central to the way it worked. Corporate reform policy assumed that educational outcomes could be similarly quantified and that the quantification would lead to better performance. Educators acknowledged the utility of metrics but believed that many of the most important educational outcomes defy simple quantification. They also thought the seeming precision of numbers was often misleading in an educational context.

There were also differences over the importance of funding. School people said that money alone wouldn't produce good results, since learning depended on so many other variables. Financial support was necessary but not sufficient to produce quality learning. In contrast, many corporate reformers seemed to have concluded that since more money didn't automatically buy better results, it wasn't really necessary. In fact, they often proposed that it was possible to reallocate funds, eliminate massive waste, and do more with the same or even less.

Perhaps the most fundamental disagreement, however, was over the goal of education. Was it first and foremost about enriching the human experience, helping people realize their potential, sustaining democracy? Or was it primarily about producing workers for business and keeping the economy competitive?

THE RISE OF CORPORATE REFORM

The historian and former undersecretary of education Diane Ravitch (2010, 2013) has provided an exhaustive examination of the business community's ongoing commitment to—and financial investment in—corporate education. But a brief summary might begin in the year 1989, when RJR Nabisco president Louis Gerstner Jr. launched a $30 million "Next Century Schools" campaign. Based on Edwards Deming's ideas, Next Century projects emphasized the importance of goal-setting, measuring progress, and entrepreneurship (Gerstner, Semerad, Doyle, & Johnston, 1994).

Almost simultaneously, the Business Roundtable, a group of top CEOs that included Gerstner, agreed on a school reform agenda. It included high expectations for all students, clear objectives, robust assessments, rewards and penalties for performance, staff training aimed at these goals, and greater use of technology. The Roundtable agreed that every state must adopt this agenda and vowed to speak with one voice to state legislatures and governors.

Members of the Roundtable pushed ahead, and shortly after the 1992 presidential election, Bill Clinton—who'd been part of the corporate reform movement when he was governor of Arkansas—endorsed the corporate agenda in the plan called Education Goals 2000. The plan rapidly won bipartisan support, the issues deserving, but never receiving, the sort of robust debate that surrounded health care, economic policy, and other "more important" topics.

By 1995, the reform agenda had evolved into nine "non-negotiables" that included state standards, tests, sanctions for failure, and better teacher education. Gerstner, who had moved on to IBM, hosted a 1996 "Education Summit" that included state governors and corporate leaders from businesses including Eastman Kodak, AT&T, Procter & Gamble, and Boeing. President Clinton told participants that "we can only do better with tougher standards and better assessment, and you [the business community] should set the standards" (Ohanian, 2006).

Gerstner subsequently co-wrote *Reinventing Education: Entrepreneurship in America's Public Schools* (1994), about RJR Nabisco's initiatives. Taking an enlightened businessperson's view, the book raised useful questions about commonly accepted practices: the way schools treated teachers like assembly-line workers, for example. In the end, however, it affirmed the virtues of the marketplace: America's longstanding public school "monopoly" should be broken. Choice and competition would force schools to improve. Forward-thinking reformers would benchmark and measure performance, apply rewards and sanctions.

The "workforce" (teachers and school administrators) would team up to satisfy "the consumer" (defined variously as the student, the parent, and big business). Students were "human capital" and teaching was the "distribution of information." Schools would compare operations the way Xerox and L.L. Bean compare inventory control. Gerstner et al. (1994) suggested they measure how much pupils learned each month, as well as how learning gains reflected dollar spending.

By the year 2000, 16 states had adopted the Roundtable platform. Worried that its initiative might stall, however, the Roundtable produced a brochure, *Assessing and Addressing the "Testing Backlash"* (2001), which offered "business coalitions and standards advocates" ammunition to fight against backsliders. In fact, most of the dissenters were actually an unorganized and politically marginal group of educators and parents who didn't want children's education reduced to numbers. At the end of the year, 28 states had signed on to standards-based reform.

By now, "business coalitions and standards advocates" included Roundtable members and governors like Jeb Bush of Florida and his brother, then-President and former Texas governor George W. Bush, as well as a range of corporations and like-minded not-for-profits. Some of the businesses, like IBM, McGraw-Hill, Pearson, and entrepreneur Christopher Whittle's Edison Schools, had substantial financial interests in testing, textbook publishing, educational technology, or for-profit schooling.

Pearson, for example, is a large multinational publisher whose North American division by itself had revenues of $2.78 billion in 2013 (Pearson, 2014). Also involved were Achieve Inc. (a pro-accountability group assembled after the 1996 Summit and affiliated with the National Governors Association), Public Agenda, the Education Coalition of the States (a national organization of state education officers), federally funded laboratories, foundations, university professors, and many newspaper editorial boards.

Few, if any, of the corporate reformers had ever worked in a public school. Like Louis Gerstner, many of them had gone to private schools. But the fact that they'd never entered a public school building as teachers or in many cases as students didn't prevent them from having firm opinions about how to reform public education. In fact, some considered their inexperience an advantage, since insiders were obviously to blame for its failure.

All this activity notwithstanding, federal intervention in public schooling had been relatively modest through the 1980s and 1990s. In 2001, however, Congress reauthorized Title I of the Elementary and Secondary Education Act of 1965. The result was the law called No Child Left Behind (NCLB). NCLB brought corporate reform up from state to national scale.

The legislation launched unprecedented federal intervention into what had been a state and local concern. For more than a century and a half, states had regulated localities, but the principle of local control had been enshrined in practice across much of the nation. A federal Office of Education hadn't even existed before the late 1800s. Subsequently, it was a backwater in the Department of the Interior, combining research and promotion initiatives with minor executive activities. It became cabinet level only in 1953, when it was sandwiched between two social services in the new Department of Health, Education, and Welfare.

Following Sputnik in 1957, the federal government took the unprecedented step of authorizing funds for nationwide teacher preparation in science and math. Not until almost a decade later, however, did Washington begin to reach more directly into local schooling. The Elementary and Secondary Education Act of 1965 reflected the Johnson administration's view that poverty and race were national issues that crossed state borders, thereby justifying federal intervention.

The new law shifted the boundary between state and federal authority for education. The section called Title I supported teacher preparation and compensatory services such as tutoring. It also funded efforts to replicate model programs and provided children with health and nutrition services. While the law affected hundreds of thousands of people, its scope, however, was limited. Federal dollars followed children below the poverty line, but participation in Title I programs remained a local option.

Meanwhile, there was continued debate over the wisdom and even the legality of direct federal involvement in schooling. A separate Department of Education (USED) wasn't created until 1979. Republicans resisted what they pictured as yet another ill-conceived foray into big government and fought the Department's existence through the 1980s, when Ronald Reagan tried but failed to abolish it.

George W. Bush entered national office in 2000, having made a reputation as "education governor" in Texas. From the start, the Bush White House saw education as central to its legacy. Staffers developed a 30-page blueprint for reform that amalgamated earlier federal proposals with plans from Florida and Texas. In effect, two of the lowest-performing states in the country were about to become the models for national policy. The most significant initiatives in the draft were high-stakes testing, school choice, and vouchers for private schools.

NO CHILD LEFT BEHIND

In 2001, a Bush adviser from Texas, Sandy Kress, shepherded the reauthorization of the Elementary and Secondary Education Act (now called No Child Left Behind) through Congress. In a political climate that made an accountability law seem inevitable and resistance politically suicidal, the nation's two large teachers' unions—the American Federation of Teachers and the National Education Association—contested only the specifics they found most objectionable. Ultimately, they agreed to a proposal to rate schools, but not teachers, by students' test scores in return for a guarantee of more federal funding.

The final version of the legislation was a bipartisan accord on principles, with regulatory specifics to be drafted later by Department of Education officials. Both major political parties and the unions claimed credit for having brought accountability to the schools. Democrats, who had successfully resisted efforts to fund vouchers, got more money for low-income schools without unilateral state control over its use. Republicans, who objected to federalized schooling, won a decentralized testing plan. States would set their own standards and choose their own exams.

Federal and state governments had gnawed away at local control for decades. NCLB was a watershed. In a *quid pro quo* that prefigured 2009's Race to the Top legislation, any state that wanted federal funding had to subject all schools within its borders to a unitary scheme of testing, as well as to federal requirements for teacher certification and curriculum selection. By 2005–06, every child in the country would be tested in grades 3 through 8 each year. Schools would then have to reach arbitrary annual scoring targets in what was called adequate yearly progress (AYP). These targets led step by step to 2013–14, when every student would be "proficient" in English and math.

To be sure no child was left behind, scores would be reported for student subgroups (the economically disadvantaged, ethnic groups, special education students, those who didn't speak English). Each subgroup, as well as each grade in every school across the country, would have to make adequate progress on schedule. If any group or subgroup didn't meet its target, the school would be "in need of improvement," a phrase the media quickly transmuted into "failing."

If it fell short of its scoring targets a second year, the school would have to submit an improvement plan to the state. If the plan didn't work after 2 more years, more serious consequences would follow. These might include involuntary personnel transfers and voluntary student transfers. Continued difficulties ultimately would lead to state takeover or to the unprecedented option of outsourcing the operation to a private corporation. Failing schools, or even whole districts, could be closed entirely.

In addition, students in failing schools could qualify for private tutoring funded by the school district. Every teacher in the country would be "highly qualified," which, among other things, meant having an academic major in the subject he or she taught. Teacher aides would need an associate's degree or would have to pass a special competency test. Programs and methods would have to be based on "scientific" research, a term that implied a standard of objectivity all but unobtainable in education. Down the road, the law's proponents contemplated new English and math tests in high school and science tests at each level.

A PARADE OF FOLLY

The law was unrealistic and illogical. Few educators thought its numerical targets were achievable. It was replete with inconsistencies, practical problems, and absurdities.

Adequate yearly progress was calculated by measuring this year's group scores against the scores of last year's group. In other words, children might have gained a year and a half of learning in 12 months, but it made no difference how much they grew from where they were before. More of them might have special needs than the children last year. More might be English language learners. None of that mattered.

A more fundamental problem was the industrial assumption that schools could produce student progress on schedule, assembly-line style, year after year. The theory was interesting; it just wasn't how people learn. Individuals acquire knowledge differently and at different rates, some incrementally, others in bursts. If teachers don't have the latitude to slow down or take unexpected turns, students may not acquire the foundation of skills and knowledge essential to more complex learning later.

NCLB's results often were unreasonable or simply puzzling. There were plenty of examples: In North Carolina, 32 schools of excellence, according to the state, failed to meet their NCLB scoring targets. In California, 317 schools that had shown tremendous gains fell short of their NCLB goals (Dillon, 2004). What to make of the inconsistency? Were the good schools really bad? Were some of the tests they used better than others? Did the exams measure the same things? Were students preparing differently for them? Who knew?

For those inclined to conspiracy theory, NCLB was a political plan whose unrealistic targets necessarily would cause huge numbers of schools to fail. The conspiracy theorists saw a plan to break teachers' unions and create school competition in order to privatize and outsource public education for less cost and more profit. But one didn't have to embrace all of these assumptions to understand that the law was about ideology, politics, and business interests as much as it was about educational merit.

NCLB invited favoritism, conflict of interest, and improprieties. Historically, states and localities had controlled most spending on educational
materials. Although Washington funded programs and services, it exerted
little influence over which specific products they bought. Textbooks were
the largest single profit center, and companies like McGraw-Hill and Pearson Scott Foresman devoted significant energy to winning contracts in
Texas and California, whose state-level adoptions influenced much of the
rest of the national market.

In the era of corporate reform, however, federal officials told corporations that they were the solution to the school problem and actively
invited them into the education marketplace. Networks of overlapping
and sometimes conflicting interests began to spill over from the state
to the federal level. When George W. Bush was governor of Texas, for
example, McGraw-Hill had been deeply involved in developing criteria for statewide text selection and subsequently won lucrative state
contracts. When he arrived in Washington, "the amount of cross-pol-
lination and mutual admiration between the Administration and [the
McGraw] empire [was] striking" (Metcalf, 2002). High-ranking executives from the publishing company transitioned in and out of positions
in the government.

Sandy Kress, the Bush education adviser, became a consultant to the
Business Roundtable and the Council of Chief State School Officers, the
organization of state school superintendents. According to Scott Parks of
The Dallas Morning News, he was a lobbyist for a think tank started by
Louis Gerstner Jr. He also lobbied for Texas business leaders who wanted
to change state education laws and consulted for Pearson on positioning
itself for the market created by NCLB. Additionally, he was a lobbyist for
Kaplan, which sold test preparation, tutoring, online coursework, and
educational materials, as well as for K-12, a business that developed and
sold a home-schooling curriculum (Parks, 2005).

In an environment where these sorts of interconnections were common, it may have been inevitable that NCLB would invite favoritism,
conflict of interest, and improprieties. A specific example was the $1 bil-
lion-a-year initiative called Reading First, wherein NCLB required states
to use education methods that were "scientifically proven" in order to
get federal money. On its face, this was a not-unreasonable effort to
control program quality and to target spending effectively. On analysis,
the proposition was problematic. As the former American Education
Research Association president James Popham (2004) pointed out, it
is seldom possible to isolate variables that affect educational outcomes
(a process essential to the scientific method). A 2007 Government Accountability Office report noted, for example, that the success of a

program reflected not just curriculum or teaching methods but factors including professional development, student time on task, and staffing levels.

When the "scientific" standard was applied to Reading First, it favored the interests of those who, for political, educational, or business reasons, supported the phonics method of reading instruction, a process of connecting sounds to letter symbols. Phonics teaching was highly structured and sometimes scripted. Studies showed that it did develop students' ability to read. The effectiveness of an alternative method, Balanced Literacy, was harder to prove, in part because teachers used multiple strategies in response to students' readiness. There was no single "it" to test or to validate. Phonics advocates consequently claimed that their method was "scientifically proven," while others were not.

To implement Reading First, the Department of Education charged an expert panel with developing the "scientific" criteria that states must meet to qualify for federal funding. At the outset, a minority of panel members claimed that the majority were known phonics advocates whose agenda was to establish standards that would disqualify other approaches. A second group of experts then determined which programs met the criteria. This group turned out to include individuals who worked for a major publisher or who had written texts or other materials that were competing for state approval (Manzo, 2005).

Early in 2006, a series of complaints and newspaper articles led the U.S. Department of Education's Inspector General to investigate. The following September, the Inspector General issued a report saying that USED officials had subverted the review panel process envisioned by Congress, intervened improperly to influence state selection of reading programs, and improperly influenced school districts in their selection of reading programs after the application process was completed (OIG, 2006). Six members of the selection panel had conflicts of interest. Among them were professors who profited from sales of their own publications; one received royalties and compensation from Pearson. Smaller publishers with research-based records of success were disqualified from competition. Big companies (Harcourt Brace, Houghton Mifflin, McGraw-Hill, and Pearson) received endorsements.

NCLB was also a technocrat's dream of the future. To comply, state bureaucracies would have to assemble, store, and sort huge amounts of data. In New York State, as a result, localities would upload those data monthly for each school and every student. Districts would have to commit time, energy, and in many cases expensive staffing to fulfill the new reporting demands.

More important, the State Education Department would have access to unprecedented amounts of information about every individual student, teacher, and school in the state. Perhaps state officials should have had the power to reach into local communities and intervene directly not only in the education but in the lives of individual children and adults. However, there was virtually no debate about the extensive data reporting, if only because few members of the public even knew about it.

Later, in 2013, many parents would protest, telling the commissioner of education to abandon plans to share student data with companies that were going to develop learning materials for sale to the state and schools (Lestch & Chapman, 2013). The State Education Department responded that Albany was more likely than localities to treat the information responsibly. Unconvinced, the protestors persevered, the initiative collapsed, and the company that was to assemble the data, inBloom, went out of business. There was nothing to prevent the Department from pursuing other questionable interlocking relationships with profit-making ventures in the future, however.

Mechanical problems also plagued the law. A whole school could "fail," for instance, if several small student subgroups didn't collectively make adequate progress over 3 years (eight Asian children one year, 10 the next, seven the third). Thirty South American children could move into a school in September, and if they didn't learn enough English within a year, the school would fail.

The law's supporters seemed to view ungainly, illogical, or unrealistic provisions like these as evidence that it just had to be fine-tuned. In practice, however, it was so shot through with problems that, pragmatically speaking, they would never be worked out.

The mechanics of funding were also a concern. Federal money would never cover the full cost of the new, open-ended, demand-driven services like the private tutoring school districts were supposed to offer if children didn't make enough progress. At least as great a concern: No Child Left Behind was significantly underfunded; it would never receive the resources that originally had been judged necessary to its success.

According to one 2004 estimate, actual Congressional allocations were $33 billion short of the amount that had been promised when the law was passed; by 2011, the estimated cumulative shortfall was $109.9 billion (NEA, 2010). As with the Individuals with Disabilities Education Act, the cost of NCLB requirements would be driven down to state and then local levels, so that other programs would receive less funding and/ or school district budgets (and taxpayer dissatisfaction) would rise.

Finally, No Child Left Behind could be seen as an absurdist comedy. More than the average bureaucratic measure, it spawned complex procedures and all-but-incomprehensible jargon that seemed entirely disassociated from its noble goals. A New York State presentation entitled "Understanding Accountability" offered the following intelligence, for example:

> An Effective AMO is the lowest PI that an accountability group of a given size can achieve in a subject for the group's PI not to be considered significantly different from the AMO for that subject. If an accountability group's PI equals or exceeds the Effective AMO, the group is considered to have made AYP. (New York State Education Department, 2003, pp. 13, 15)

Delphic utterings like these could sound impressively technical and important, as if they reflected some kind of higher science, which may have been part of the point. What normal person would try to extract meaning from them, let alone challenge them? Fortunately for the average citizen, attempting to interpret them was the school administrator's unhappy lot.

The wording of the state's guidance and the ideas behind it were at once excruciatingly awful and strangely fascinating. What did the language mean? What did the convolutions say about the mindset behind the law? This was how to make sure kids got an education? Did any of it have to do with placing young people in the care of inspiring, devoted teachers?

And more broadly speaking, NCLB was a treasure chest of wonderful irony. Beneath a cloak of free-enterprise rhetoric, it resembled nothing more than the kind of central planning, complete with performance targets and mass production techniques, that had long characterized the late Soviet Union. To compound the weirdness, an administration that trumpeted its commitment to small government was promoting massive bureaucratic expansion that would cause states to track the progress and to certify the individual achievement of every student in the country.

THE TRIUMPH OF CORPORATE REFORM

As the full implications of this unprecedented shift in government authority began to come clear in the early 2000s, a handful of governors and state legislatures briefly resisted. Independent-minded Utah threatened to disregard the legislation. The rock-ribbed New Englanders of Connecticut sued the federal government for mandating a program it wouldn't fully fund.

But visible resistance dwindled quickly. The majority of state governments, big business, newspapers, the White House, and the U.S. Department of Education were on board. Especially in some troubled school districts, educators bought into a plan that seemed to chart a clear course through a sea of educational dysfunction and promised added funding.

Skeptics, meanwhile, were a loose aggregation of advocacy groups, some university professors and parents, and larger numbers of school administrators and teachers. While many of them actually had experience with real students in real schools, they were on the defensive from the start.

The corporate approach might have been a superficial quick fix, a bureaucrat's idea of quality. Nonetheless, the skeptics were unable to influence unfolding events. Many resorted to the tactics of the powerless. They acceded to the inevitable, subverted it where possible, tried to find silver linings in dark clouds, and salvaged what they could.

No Child Left Behind had been in effect for seven years when the Obama administration took office in January 2009. America confronted ongoing challenges associated with climate change, economic globalization, terrorism, and geopolitical and religious tensions. Candidate Obama had pictured education as the solution to these dilemmas. Following the financial collapse of 2008, however, his most pressing concerns were economic.

Once in office, the new administration differed with its predecessor on issues from health care to terrorism. Nonetheless, its education policies turned out to be remarkable for their consistency with the Bush approach. A new Department of Education Secretary, Arne Duncan, talked about the value of teaching. In practice, he doubled down on the corporate strategy that was now more than 2 decades old.

The Department would continue to quantify goals, measure results, apply rewards and sanctions, and promote competition among schools and teachers. Accordingly, it directed $3.1 billion to school reform in a new initiative, "Race to the Top," that required states to commit themselves to Washington's reform agenda. To "win" federal funding, a state had to support charter schools, high-stakes testing, teacher evaluations tied to students' test results, and other familiar elements of the corporate strategy.

No Child Left Behind's limitations had been evident from the start, but it was a full decade before Secretary Duncan announced, in August, 2011, that he was overriding its core requirement: that 100% of students be proficient in math and reading by 2013–14. About 38,000 of the nation's 100,000 public schools had failed to meet their scoring targets in 2010; the Secretary predicted the number would rise to 80,000 in 2011.

He called the law "a slow-motion train wreck" that was getting in the way of the states' efforts to raise standards (Dillon, 2011).

Unhappily, Duncan's decision didn't represent an acknowledgment of fundamental flaws in either NCLB or the corporate approach more generally. It was yet another technical response to what the Department of Education continued to see as the law's mechanical problems. As Gene Wilhoit, executive director of the Council of Chief State School Officers, said, NCLB was "identifying such an outlandish number of schools as failures, it was losing credibility" (Dillon, 2011). The response was to try to fix the clockwork.

Corporate reform was unsound and its negative results were evident. Its insufficiencies should have led officials to reassess it from the bottom up. Instead, when the school doors opened in September and children came back to class, its shade roamed the halls undisturbed, largely unquestioned by anyone who could have made a difference

CHAPTER 5

GRADING CORPORATE REFORM

I've never heard a school or college graduate mention test scores when she described the value of her education. I have heard people say they learned to love science or history or literature, and I've heard them credit teachers with having changed the way they thought. By definition, an excellent education is distinctive, qualitatively richer and stronger than the kind of learning numbers measure. It helps students to become highly effective thinkers, resolute problem-solvers, and contributors. It explores the limits of individual potential and changes lives for the better.

These aren't corporate reform's concerns. At best, it drags education toward a low average. It does a middling job of providing children a solid academic foundation. It actually undermines efforts to unleash human ingenuity and imagination. With credit for its sometimes good intentions, it is worth a "C." At least as important, the approach falls well short of what other nations are doing to ready their young for the challenges of the global community. In that sense, it has launched America into a race to the bottom and merits a grade of "D" or worse.

IMPACT ON TEACHING

One of corporate reform policy's stated objectives is to use high-stakes tests, test data, and sanctions to improve teaching. The underlying logic is a closed loop: Test scores are the measure of an education. Punishment for poor scores (and less commonly, reward for good ones) will cause teaching to improve. When teaching improves, scores will ascend. That will mean children's education is better.

There are obvious difficulties with this reasoning. Standardized tests do not evaluate many important aspects of learning. Punishment may not improve instruction; it can cause teachers to adopt methods that are expedient and merely strategic. Higher scores may not mean that valuable learning is occurring. They can merely reflect test preparation.

Nonetheless, understanding that the strategy's underlying assumptions are shaky, what can we deduce about the impact of high-stakes standardized testing on teaching?

Each spring, school districts across New York State upload the latest round of test scores to so-called "data cubes" that reside somewhere in Education Department cyberspace. Score reports return in the fall. This process is replicated across the country.

In theory, teachers analyze the results to help each child learn better. In practice, this exercise can be revealing, but sometimes it's just puzzling.

Students miss questions for no evident reason. Perfectly logical responses are "wrong" according to the scoring booklet. Children leave items blank. Nobody can be sure why. Perhaps they are bored. Sometimes, their in-class work shows that they understand the material but they answer incorrectly anyway.

In addition, the seeming objectivity of the numbers conceals significant imprecision. Poorly worded questions, statistical error, and "noise" (an exam was administered in a hot, humid room) make results less meaningful than they seem. In short, and for many reasons, it can be hard to know what to make of the results.

In New York, to complicate matters, results come back months after children took the tests. Do the numbers from the spring reflect what they know in the fall? It's difficult to say. Even more troubling: Test security concerns limit the information teachers get back about each child. In the self-proclaimed State of Learning, teachers can't use the results to evaluate what individual students know.

Albany does provide more information about how whole classes or grades perform, so it is possible to look for patterns of right and wrong responses. If a number of students miss the same question, for example, their teachers can consider a change in curriculum, so the next year's group may understand the topic better.

Inconveniently, however, responses don't always distribute themselves so obligingly. Teachers discover that right and wrong answers occur at random. One student misses items 2 and 7; another, items 13 and 22, and so on. Even when the answers do fall into patterns, teachers may still face a dilemma.

A significant number of children miss question 7, about the quadrilateral. It turns out that they studied the topic in May, after they took the test, so there is no reason they should have done well. Their teachers discuss whether to cover the topic earlier this coming year, in March, before the test.

If they shift the curriculum calendar, they will have less time to build the math background that will help children understand the concept. If they do not, memorization and test prep may enable more youngsters to get the right answer, but they will be less likely to understand why it is right. What will happen? Remember that in a high-stakes environment, a significant percentage of each teacher's performance rating must be based on students' scores.

In some cities and states, newspapers decide to put these ratings online. With the stakes even higher, how much class time will faculty invest in helping children develop a strong sense of what numbers mean? How much time will they spend investigating interesting questions in math? How much time will they devote to targeted test prep?

As the pressure for high scores grows, teaching becomes more strategic. Teachers cover the content they think will be tested. They have students answer questions from past tests and do assignments that mirror possible test questions. They also teach test-taking tricks, such as how to improve the odds of guessing correctly. The higher the stakes, the more pronounced the tendency to adopt these strategies (Blazer, 2011).

In addition, teachers concentrate on "low-hanging fruit" (students on the cusp of passing), and they spend less time on those well below the bar. To cover everything that might be tested, they lecture and use methods that are more "efficient" than discussion, inquiry, or experimentation. They narrow the curriculum: Reading, writing, and math displace social studies, science, and the arts. These effects are especially pronounced in low-income communities (Blazer, 2011).

After observing thousands of classrooms in urban schools, University of Wisconsin professor Martin Haberman has described "a tightly controlled routine in which teachers dispense, and then test students on, factual information; assign seatwork; and punish noncompliance. . . . It is a regimen in which learners can 'succeed' without becoming either involved or thoughtful—and it is noticeably different from the questioning, discovering, arguing, and collaborating that is more common (though by no means universal) among students in suburban and private schools. . . . 'The overly directive, mind-numbing, anti-intellectual acts' that pass for teaching in most urban schools 'not only remain the coin of the realm but have become the gold standard'" (quoted in Kohn, 2011).

The point, as Scarsdale's middle school principal Michael McDermott would say, is not that standardized tests have no instructional value. It is that their value is limited. They can help identify trends, provoke useful questions, or validate the findings of other assessments. But their results can be equivocal or inconclusive. They may add little to what teachers already know from student conferences, written work, or class observations. They can have important undesirable side effects. And these side effects tend to be pronounced in less advantaged communities. The issue is one of cost and benefit.

CREATING ECONOMIES

Corporate reform can also be about improving productivity, a process of seeing how little money is needed to produce the best test scores. An objective is to save money by stripping schools clean of what often is portrayed as bloated bureaucracy, as well as by controlling "unsustainable" salaries and benefits. The line of logic leads ultimately to the view that since taxpayers don't get value for the generous funding they pour into public schools now, there is no reason to spend more. In fact, they should spend less.

So, for example, Kenneth Adams (2008), president of the New York Business Council, fulminates that the Empire State has "the highest per pupil education spending in this country, nearly $19,000 per student, 63% above the national average. Yet, we're 33rd in the nation in eighth grade math scores and not much better in other . . . measures." Governor Andrew Cuomo uses the same rationale to justify his plan to cap taxes: The state could get better results for less money, like neighboring Massachusetts.

These kinds of arguments are common and problematic. To start, Adams arranges facts to support his theory, overstating the cost of education in New York by almost $2,000 per student. In 2008, it was closer to $17,000 than $19,000 according to the U.S. Bureau of the Census (2010). He also ignores the fact that New York's school districts operate in a state with the third-highest cost of living in the nation, after the District of Columbia and Hawaii (Aten, Figueroa, Martin, 2012). The general labor force is the second-highest paid in the nation.

His argument also ignores other important facts. New York has higher costs than many other states for legitimate reasons. For instance, state law makes New York's special education programs among the most robust—and costly—in the country. In New York, local school budgets fund the state retirement system, while in Massachusetts, the Commonwealth does. Neither do Massachusetts school districts (or the state) pay for teachers' Social Security. In New York, schools must pay for student transportation, athletics, and other extracurricular activities. In Massachusetts, districts can charge user fees for these activities.

Schools in New York also face a bigger challenge than those in Massachusetts. The percent of Empire State children in poverty (21%) is roughly the national average, appreciably higher than the 14% in its northern neighbor (McCartney, 2011). In fact, given the strong correlation between students' economic background and test scores, New Yorkers may be getting a reasonable or even better-than-average return on their investment in public schools. Considering all results instead of looking selectively at the 8th grade, reading and math scores for the Empire State are at or above the national average.

International comparisons are similarly problematic. U.S. per-pupil expenditures are relatively high and test results middling. Corporate reformers sometimes argue that America could cut costs and do as well as higher-scoring nations. But schools in different countries provide different services: Special-needs programs aren't all the same, for instance, and schools overseas are less likely to have robust athletic programs—or any athletic programs at all. There are important differences in poverty levels, hunger, and second-language populations. High-cost items like health care and retirement benefits may be in school budgets in the United States, but may be considered national responsibilities elsewhere.

IMPROVING EFFICIENCY

The corporate reformers' interest in economy often coincides with an interest in using technology to create efficiencies. For example, former New York City schools chancellor Joel Klein has described a future of technology-laden schools where a few highly trained career teachers impart important material and less expensive aides monitor routine learning. Another vision has computers tracking and prescribing the education of students who get services from approved providers: a math tutor here, an autonomous athletic program there, an English class in a traditional school, some online learning at home.

There's no shortage of imagined education utopias. But is it a good idea to split learning neatly into complex and simple activities? Is it even possible? In math, young children use wooden or plastic blocks to count; simultaneously, they develop a sense of what numbers mean and how they work. With great respect for what an excellent teacher aide can do, what parent wants an aide to be primarily responsible for "monitoring" this "simple" activity? Who wouldn't rather have a teacher who's been trained to understand the child's thinking and to explain the subject in a way that makes sense to her?

More broadly, where does a vision of consumer-driven education lead? Should buyer preference or professional expertise determine what an education is? Should Americans share some common educational experience, or should there be as many educations as there are children, depending on what parents think? If we have 50 million different educations, how do future citizens learn to live and work together? What holds us together as a people?

COMPETITION AND TEACHER RANKINGS

The corporate agenda also envisions a future in which teacher rankings, merit pay, and charter schools motivate people, drive out the weakest performance, and improve what's left. I'll discuss charter schools in Chapter 6. For now, let us examine, first, how competition relates to teacher motivation and, second, the practical limitations of corporate-style evaluation systems in education.

To begin, the urge to compete isn't necessarily the only thing or even the main thing that motivates the people who enter teaching. Many are driven by an idealistic desire to make a difference or to contribute. Others want to nurture their students or to develop positive relationships. Some are averse to risk or function best in a secure environment. Competition is not necessarily congruent with these predispositions, and it can be at odds with some of them. Some teachers actually find it de-motivating.

Second, precise numerical teacher ratings and rankings are not credible from a technical standpoint. They are the product of algorithms whose results may be mathematically correct without accurately describing the quality of a teacher's work. Especially problematic is the effort to translate students' test scores into teacher ratings. As the National Research Council (NRC, 2009) has observed, inherent data problems make such correlations "far too unstable to be considered fair or reliable" (p. 10).

Absent teacher ratings that are both mathematically correct *and* meaningful, there is no responsible way to rank people relative to one another on a numerical scale. It is possible to draw empirical distinctions on a gross level: between the strongest and weakest performers, for example. But are there really meaningful differences between number 20, number 25, and number 30?

More to the point, why try to make such distinctions? Too often, the effort turns into a hair-splitting exercise that is not worth the cynicism, division, and bickering that it breeds. More important, how is it necessary to the main work at hand? Most faculties resemble the snake that ate the elephant: a small group of recognized stars at one end, a relatively small group of dimmer lights at the other. In the large middle are the rest of us, with varied strengths and skills.

In most cases, therefore, the way to lift the collective quality of a faculty is not to fire low-performing outliers, although they certainly require attention. Rather, it is to improve the effectiveness of the middle by involving each person in a continuous effort to achieve a personal best. That is accomplished by developing individual plans for professional growth and then providing direct, ongoing feedback about where and why performance is effective and might improve. This feedback should be anchored in evidence—gleaned from classroom visits, student work, teaching materials, and teachers' reflections in areas such as planning, classroom environment, teaching methods, and professionalism (Danielson, 2007).

While precise numerical ratings and rankings are not necessary to this work, supervisors can make judgments about whether performance is distinguished, proficient, developing, or unsatisfactory. Where serious shortcomings in academic background or observable classroom weaknesses are concerned, that is a relatively simple task.

More difficult to address are problems involving judgment or human relations, ones that are more subjective, often hard to observe, and less easy to define. An example: One of the most memorable classes I have ever seen was a wide-ranging exchange about the history and spirit of the 1920s. I walked out wishing I could have taken the whole course.

What I didn't know for some time was that the teacher demeaned her slower students when I wasn't there. The challenge was to figure out that a problem existed, to get students and parents to come forward, to wade through claims and counterclaims about what actually happened in the absence of an objective observer, and to develop hard evidence that her behavior was unacceptable.

Why try to decide whether she was a 2, 4, or 7?

COMPETITION AND MERIT PAY

The logical end of performance ratings is a system that rewards and punishes people for the quality of their efforts. It is an approach that works in the private sector because productive employees create capital, and capital expands as productivity and/or markets grow. Profit then gives the corporation a pool of money large enough to reward its effective employees.

In public education, funding comes from taxes; productive teachers don't generate more income for the "corporation." Most communities tax themselves only enough to compete in a regional marketplace. Tax growth bears a rough relationship to growth in the cost of living. As a result, historically, funds for discretionary expenditures have been modest.

Still, before the advent of unions and before freedom of information laws made salaries public, pay-for-performance was more common. Because funds were so limited, merit awards tended to be very modest and/ or available only to a relatively small number of people. Often, therefore, the presumed merits of merit pay were more theoretical than real.

Without evaluation criteria that were both objective and meaningful enough to put teachers' ratings beyond reasonable dispute, furthermore, school boards wrangled over details of the system and faculty looked askance at the results. In theory, they didn't know what one another made. In practice, salary information leaked out, and perceived inequities fueled cynicism and friction, often as much because people felt devalued as because of the actual dollars involved.

It was hard experience with these realities that led a Scarsdale board member from the early 1950s to describe merit pay as "a hornet's nest." They were also why many school boards ultimately concluded that the system's presumed advantages weren't worth the conflict and the morale problems they generated. The result was a salary schedule that rewarded experience and formal education, objective criteria everyone could agree on.

With all that said, one of the more interesting aspects of merit pay was that there was not and is not clear evidence that it actually improved teaching or learning, if only because "it" could take so many different forms (Marsh, Rothstein, Figlio, & Guthrie, 2011). In the era of corporate reform, nonetheless, some school districts determinedly headed down the merit path again.

The benefits of merit pay are not as compelling as its supporters may believe, but if the concept is to work at all, the criteria for awards must be clear in advance. They also must be concrete and meaningful. So, for instance, a teacher might be recognized for pursuing a particular line of research or for developing his skills in a particular area of expertise.

Further, since teaching is a craft that improves through collaboration, a successful merit plan should reward it. If you are competing with your neighbor, why help him? You could improve his rating and his pay at your own expense.

Finally, a successful merit plan must draw on a pool of money large enough to give meaningful rewards to all who meet the specified criteria. If the odds say only a handful of people can succeed or if the incentive is small, why take the plan seriously? Why play?

IMPROVING LEARNING

The most important promise of the corporate reform strategy is that it, and high-stakes testing in particular, will improve learning. But after more than a quarter of a century, it is far from clear that it does.

In the early 2000s, a series of "dueling studies" analyzed and re-analyzed test data, including results of the NAEP. Often, the opposing views reflected differences between two schools of experts. Some were more traditional researchers who tended to treat data cautiously, in terms not only of what they might reveal, but also of their limitations. Others were relative newcomers who thought that the "science" of economet-rics could lead them to relatively conclusive judgments about academic progress and quality. There turned out to be no definitive evidence that high-stakes testing achieved its main goal, raising "fundamental ques-tions about why we even have federal and state policies that exact strong penalties for students, teachers, and schools when such policies are an-chored in so little knowledge about what works in improving teaching and learning" (Cuban, 2005, p.39).

NAEP is America's sole independent nationwide measure of student learning. Schools and teachers do not prep their pupils specifically for it because it is not tied to a specific curriculum, and it is not high-stakes. As a result, it comes as close as possible to being an impartial assessment of whether learning is improving. Between 1990 and 2005, 4th-grade NAEP scores in math rose 25 points, while 8th-grade math scores rose 16 points. Gains were particularly strong in the South. And in 2002, former U.S. secretary of education Margaret Spellings triumphantly heralded these results as evidence that NCLB's high-stakes testing strategy was a success (Manzo & Cavanaugh, 2005).

The claim was patently specious; the law couldn't have been respon-sible for 12 years' worth of growth that had occurred before it existed. So the chair of the board that set policy for NAEP, Darvin M. Winick, offered an alternative explanation: The trend might reflect corporate-style re-forms at the state level after 1985, especially in the South (Dobbs, 2005). But that analysis was also questionable.

According to long-term NAEP data, results actually had started to improve in the 1970s, before either corporate reform or NCLB existed. As Daniel Koretz, Shattuck Professor of Education at Harvard, observed, scores had declined in the 1960s in both low- and high-achieving schools all across the country, as well as in neighboring Canada. An equally wide-spread increase followed in the 1970s (Koretz, 1987). Especially notewor-thy was the fact that African Americans had begun to close the achievement gap. There was no clear reason. As Stanford's Linda Darling-Hammond theorized in 2001(see Chapter 2), it may have been Johnson-era anti-poverty legislation and educational reforms. Or possibly, as Koretz suggested, a variety of complex factors inside or outside of schools—many of them undetermined—could have been at work (Koretz, 1987).

In fact, long-term NAEP math and reading scores for younger children had improved starting in the 1970s up through the latest testing in the 2000s. Meanwhile, scores for 17-year-olds, the oldest students to take NAEP, remained essentially flat throughout the entire period. African Americans gained the most on White children in the years before *A Nation at Risk*; after 1985, the achievement gap for 17-year-olds remained essentially the same.

In short, there was some progress over 40 years, but the results of corporate-style metrics and accountability in particular were neither clear nor impressive.

More specifically, a 2011 National Research Council (NRC) report found that high-stakes testing had only a slight impact on student performance (Hout & Elliott, 2011). And as Koretz and Hamilton noted, "Evidence about the effects of high-stakes testing . . . indicates that the gains in scores . . . often generalize poorly (or not at all) to other tests of the same domain, raising doubts about the extent to which these gains provide valid evidence of improved student performance" (Koretz & Hamilton, 2003, p. 2).

Although high-stakes testing was not clearly associated with improved learning, it did correlate with higher dropout rates. As early as 1999, an NRC study said that

> much of the existing research shows that high-stakes tests are associated with higher dropout rates. Kreutzer et al. (1989) compared the testing activities in the 10 states with the highest dropout rates and the 10 states with the lowest dropout rates. They found that nine of the 10 states with the highest dropout rates had high-stakes graduation tests, and none of the states with low dropout rates used the tests for high-stakes purposes. (Heubert & Hauser, 1999, p. 174)

A little over a decade later, in 2011, the NRC reconfirmed that high-stakes "high school exit exam programs . . . decrease the rate of high school graduation without increasing achievement" (Hout & Eliott, 2011, p. 4).

Among interventions that do work, according to research, are higher salaries to attract better teachers, staff development, early childhood education, and approaches such as Reading Recovery, an intensive form of instruction at the early grades (Darling-Hammond, 2001). But corporate reform instead has embraced what University of Cambridge professor

Michael McIntyre (2002) has called "audit culture," trying to regulate better education into being.

As McIntyre says, audit culture assumes that people can't be trusted, and it employs a regressing series of controls to force them to do their jobs. For example, NCLB's tests could be considered a first level of control. Its ascending scoring targets were a second level ("The auditors must be audited"). Its written improvement plans were a third. Subsequent levels involved student transfers, administrative removals, and, ultimately, state takeover. At some point, of course, the question was the one a dog faces when he runs after a bus: What does he do if he catches it?

Undeniably, the corporate strategy of adopting legislation, setting performance standards, and embracing a "shape-up-or-ship-out" ambience forced change. But applied indiscriminately to the complex problems of public education, it proved to be "incoherent, wasteful and socially crippling," in McIntyre's (2002) words. Old organizational dynamics persisted, evolved, and thwarted meaningful improvement. Consequences couldn't be anticipated. Results varied, and they often undermined quality education.

GLOBAL COMPETITIVENESS

Historically, as we've seen, America's system of educational opportunity was exceptional. In the United Kingdom, a national examination system screened children out of advanced education; through the mid-1900s, relatively few stayed in school beyond the age of 16. Germany's vocational schools pre-empted advanced academic study for most. All French children studied a national curriculum; rigid tracking started well before high school.

In the 1800s and 1900s, these European models of education shaped schooling worldwide. Colonies like Singapore adopted the education systems of their conquerors. In Japan, schools tracked children heavily during their middle years, and college admission was based on high-stakes tests. Recently, I talked with a 12-year-old who had been raised in Hawaii before her family moved back to Japan. Still struggling to adjust, she had been placed in the lowest academic level. She had little hope of attending a Japanese university.

In contrast, and despite its shortcomings, the decentralized American system of schooling of the 20th century offered multiple second chances. It was common to sort students into different academic levels, but a single exam was less likely to determine individual fates. Teachers often had latitude to adapt local curriculum and instruction to the needs and interests of youngsters in their classes, and students could take alternative routes to a high school diploma. A range of 2- and 4-year colleges and universities made higher education widely available. This loosely coupled system was well-suited for a society known for its individualism, innovation, and social mobility.

In the last decades of the 1900s, however, global economic change and the rise of second- and third-world countries caused many nations overseas to reassess. The United Kingdom made a concerted effort to increase its staying-on rate, and more students went to university. Singapore decided to use its geographic location and human capital to become the western Pacific's economic hub. In the 1960s, its goal was to give all citizens a sound elementary education. Later, it shifted emphasis to preparing workers for technical jobs. In 1997, the Ministry of Education adopted plans to create a workforce for a knowledge-based economy.

Finland also re-evaluated its prospects in the 1970s. A small country whose main resource was people, it also embarked on a long-term plan to improve its education system. Now a top scorer in the Programme for International Student Assessment (PISA), the nation emerged as a global poster child for education reform. It didn't use standardized tests for accountability. The school day and year were short, and children were expected to be children. The government adopted clear learning goals, but teachers had considerable latitude in approach. Most important, the nation recruited the top 10% of its college graduates to teach, limited admission to schools of education, and improved teacher preparation radically.

China and India are not among today's top world scorers, but they may not need to be. For example, China can develop an academic elite by directing the most talented 25% of its 1.3 billion people to advanced study, then streaming everyone else off to other training. Assuming it does, it will have more highly educated scientists, engineers, physicians, and professors than a United States that somehow might manage to educate every single child to the same high level.

Ironically, however, other nations still see America as a model. Not the America of corporate reform, No Child Left Behind, or Race to the Top, but the country that has long produced independent, innovative thinkers. In fact, Pacific Rim nations like Singapore and China have invested substantially in bringing educators to see schools in the United States. In the past two years, Scarsdale hosted representatives from both nations, the Chinese observers for several months.

Why? A visiting Singapore Ministry of Education official observed that she is sometimes asked why anyone from her country would bother to visit America, where students' international test scores are lower. Her answer is that whatever the scores may be, America produces Nobel Prize winners. Singapore wants to learn how.

The United States, meanwhile, is headed back in the opposite direction; our students now take more standardized tests than those in any other country in the world. To be sure, international parallels are tricky. Nations like Finland and Singapore are very different from the United States, and it would be a mistake to try to transfer their reforms here, wholesale. Still, we might productively ask what we can learn from others.

In 2010, an Organisation for Economic Co-operation and Development study found that the world's most improved education systems shared certain characteristics. Chief among them were comprehensive efforts to build educators' skills, assess student progress, improve data systems, revise standards and curriculums, and structure appropriate rewards. Specific schemes like high-stakes testing, school choice, or merit pay were not critical. What did make a difference was a commitment to develop professional capacity, to improve assessment, to make better information available to the professionals, and so on.

Further, systems at different stages of development employed different kinds of strategies. For example, those on the road from fair to good were more apt to mandate specific teacher training programs. Those journeying from good to excellent gave teachers flexibility to devise their own plans. The world's most improved systems recognized the limits of compliance strategies and understood the value of moving on to other approaches when they could (Mourshad, Chijioke, & Barber, 2010).

Also, it's instructive that many of the highest-performing countries in the world esteem teaching. They do their best to attract top talent, reward practitioners, and value professional development. Some, like our diverse, if less populous, neighbor Canada, are less sharply divided between rich and poor. Often, they also have stronger safety nets for children from backgrounds where poverty, health, and family stability are problems.

If we want our schools and our children to be global leaders, we have to think in terms like these. How can we offset the gap between rich and poor and address the effects of poverty? How can we best foster the highly developed skills and learning that an advanced, knowledge-based society depends on? As Cambridge's Michael McIntyre (2002) says, crucial to the development of these capacities are unmeasurables such as curiosity, interest, enthusiasm, and room for creativity.

Ingenuity and creativity, our traditional strong suits, can compensate for other nations' size and drive. But if America is to sustain and build on these strengths, we need to educate our young people to think well, to be curious and inventive. We have to pursue the dream of individual potential fulfilled.

CHAPTER 6

CHARTER SCHOOLING

When I discussed corporate reform in Chapter 5, I said that belief in metrics and accountability has led to the over-quantification of education and to an undue reliance on high-stakes testing. I also proposed that the familiar business principle of minimizing investment for maximum profit is consistent with our oft-grudging approach to funding education.

The third article of corporate faith—that competition produces quality—gave rise to the charter school movement. Supported by public funds, charter schools operate independent of the regular public system, usually with far less regulation. Often, they also have added financial support from businesses or foundations.

Theoretically, charters free education entrepreneurs to create break-the-mold schools, which drive others to improve. In practice, some charters are highly regimented and traditional. Others resemble community or alternative schools from the 1960s and 1970s. Parent satisfaction tends to be high, but on the whole, student achievement is no better than it is in the regular system. Charter school practices have not transformed district public schools.

There is more than a little irony in a corporate strategy of deregulating and generously financing charter schools while over-regulating and underfunding those in the traditional system. If added resources and fewer rules are the recipe for better performance in some cases, why unwaveringly impose compliance and audit in others? Why make it difficult for district schools to compete?

Another inconsistency of corporate reform is that when businesses work directly in schools, their emphasis isn't usually on accountability or trying to minimize their financial investment. Instead, they're likely to commit real money to support sustained teacher education, professional teamwork, technology, and school–community involvement.

After Louis Gerstner moved to IBM, for example, the company joined hands with the Chicago Education Alliance, a group that included the city school district, the teachers' union, and universities. It underwrote online teacher collaboration, mentoring, training, and inservice education.

It also supported new hands-on curriculums and promoted connections between secondary and postsecondary education.

Evaluations of the initiative were positive, but were any of the corporate movement's signature elements—accountability, economy, or competition—responsible? When it dug into the work of change, IBM invested in academic infrastructure and in building professional cultures to support teaching and learning. In fact, the company took pride in its multimillion-dollar commitment to these kinds of efforts (IBM, 2001). Also, as Harvard University's Richard Elmore said, the partnership's success reflected the fact that it had engaged "the best academic minds in Chicago, who are the best academic minds in the United States" (Ravitch & Elmore, 2002, pp. 378–379).

Diane Ravitch, originally a corporate reform advocate, became one of the movement's most ardent critics. In *The Death and Life of the Great American School System* (2010), she describes it as an experiment in short-sighted quick fixes. The main beneficiaries, she says, are entrepreneurs and financiers who, among other things, operate for-profit schools and sell the "three T's": tests, texts, and technology. The financial stakes are in the billions of dollars.

Ravitch discusses an early 2000s reform effort in San Diego called the "Blueprint for Student Success." School district leaders mandated teaching methods, emphasized accountability, demanded higher test scores, and advocated firing principals, fighting the teachers' union, and opening charter schools. Some elementary-grade test scores rose, but the plan alienated many of the teachers whose cooperation was necessary for long-term success. As San Diego employed these approaches in its main system, meanwhile, it took a very different tack with its charter schools.

HIGH TECH HIGH SCHOOL

High Tech High nestles in a large building on the former grounds of the U.S. Navy Training Center in San Diego. Founded in 1999, the school's goal is to prepare graduates for local jobs in science and technology. Hence, the name "High Tech"; electronic paraphernalia aren't central to its day-to-day operations.

In the mid-1990s, San Diego's Business Roundtable and its Economic Development Corporation decided to create a high school that would work according to modern business principles. They hired Larry Rosenstock, head of the federal New Urban Schools Project, to be its founding CEO. "Design" and "team" would be key principles. Given the corporate language, one might have expected the result to be a model of metrics and accountability.

Instead, High Tech High is a neo-progressive lighthouse that reflects the influence of the Coalition of Essential Schools, as well as school-to-work programs. The Coalition was the brainchild of the late Theodore Sizer, who was head of the education department at Brown University in the 1980s. The Coalition's 10 commonsense principles subsequently became so ingrained in the language—if not necessarily the practice—of public schools that it was easy to forget their origin.

For instance, Coalition schools embraced the premise that schools should teach a core of essential skills and knowledge instead of trying to cover huge amounts of content. Decisions about curriculum, the use of time, teaching materials, and methods should be in the hands of the principal and staff. The governing metaphor should be student-as-worker rather than teacher-as-deliverer-of-instructional-services (Coalition of Essential Schools, 2015). These principles are clearly evident at High Tech High.

School-to-work initiatives draw heavily on John Dewey's premise that practical experience makes learning meaningful. Therefore, schools should try to link students' academic work with real-world applications. Job shadowing or internships should connect school learning to businesses and the professions. High Tech High, says a staff member, is about students, subject integration, hands and minds, school and work.

The school selects its 500 students through a lottery that is intended to ensure they'll reflect the makeup of the city. The faces are African American, Hispanic, Asian, and Anglo. Despite their ethnic diversity, the kids are more middle class than their counterparts across the city, according to one teacher. Eighty percent go to 4-year universities, well above the norm at most nonselective urban schools.

Winding down the main axis of the building, a central atrium showcases handsome science- and math-oriented student projects. A suspended wooden bridge illustrates principles of compression. A hand crank moves chains that connect 10 or 20 bike wheels on a wall. Other walls are covered with brightly colored murals or are thick with framed student paintings in reds and vivid blues. Supported crosswise by metal trusses, the ceiling contains a grid of light-filled, industrial-style windows. Slung below it lengthwise are long, narrow metal trays that carry blue computer cabling.

Charter status means the school can choose faculty without state credentials. Some, like the 24-year-old who started out in Teach for America and then worked in New York City, are trained teachers. Others, like the former merchant seaman, used to be engineers or scientists or in business.

The school recruits on Craigslist; the interview process includes a sort of speed-dating-with-students exercise. Not only does the mix make for an interesting faculty; life experience allows teachers to benchmark student learning against real-world expectations.

In more established schools, faculties typically conform to "the rule of thirds." One third readily embraces new ideas. A third is willing to be convinced. The rest are reluctant. Only when the second third is ready to go, can the school move. Even then, some teachers are likely to resist or stay behind. At High Tech High, the roughly 40 faculty members have been chosen for qualities that specifically include enterprise and willingness to take risks. Because the school is explicit about its interest in innovation, most, if not all, are on board with change, according to Rob Riordan (personal communication, October 21, 2009), a sort of provost who calls himself "the Emperor of Rigor."

In their first 2 years, students take "exploration courses" and carry out teacher-designed projects. Explorations might involve fieldwork or community service, but basically they are opportunities to reach into a world that opens onto the Pacific. In a space defined by a glass wall that extends about halfway to the ceiling, 15 or 20 ninth-graders are making Styrofoam plane models. They're exploring basic physical principles and putting them into practice. Each plane has to carry an egg. If the plane crashes and the egg breaks, they haven't gotten the lesson.

Projects are distinctive elements of a High Tech High education, and they are the heart of the curriculum. Teachers invent extended learning activities that cut across disciplines—marrying math, science, and social studies or art, English, and science, for example. Operating within parameters that loosen as they grow older, students assume increasing responsibility for initiating and carrying out the work.

One example is the Bay Project, an extended, multi-year study that's being conducted in partnership with the Navy and the San Diego Bay Authority. Currently, students are examining the impact of invasive species on marine ecology. They identify the small critters that have attached themselves to rope strung in the bay, learning about how the animals work and what they do. The data they produce become part of the professional analysis that is at the center of the study.

I ask a blond, spiky-haired boy what larger problem the research is trying to solve. He says he doesn't know, but he's sure it's a worthwhile effort. Still, he continues, the bivalves he's studying are really cool. He proceeds in impressive technical language to describe their genetic and biological structure and the place they're forging for themselves in the ecosystem. As a former English major, I take it on faith that he knows what he's talking about.

This kind of project-centered learning obviously differs from the classroom lecture and Socratic question–response. Students pursue long-term assignments that mimic real-world tasks or address authentic problems. The young man I met seems typical: He's an active and inquisitive learner, engaged in his studies, a team player. With the teacher out of the room, he and his classmates collaborate in a relaxed but purposeful way, much like adults in an office or lab. The students seem motivated and self-directed and it's evident that they like to learn.

According to one faculty member, a strength of the project approach is that teachers who used to be professional designers or managers or researchers can develop courses that draw on their experience with real-world problems, as well as on the personal passions they developed in their years of applied work. Once they've created their curriculums, they crosswalk them against California's state standards to be sure they're meeting its learning goals.

The project approach also enables the school to keep classes heterogeneous; students are not separated into groups of higher or lower ability. As a result, everyone has access to the same courses, and the system doesn't discourage anyone from trying more challenging work. Teachers design activities that vary in difficulty or plan a single activity with different elements. "There are lots of entry points to the subject matter and lots of ways to show what you've learned," says Riordan (personal communication).

The project approach also enhances school culture and student life. Many of the kids come from schools where students self-segregate along ethnic and racial lines. Here, the heterogeneous grouping, the emphasis on teamwork, and efforts to develop a strong sense of school ownership all increase communication and minimize artificial divisions and cliques, Riordan says.

Nonetheless, project centeredness has its drawbacks. Despite the instructional differentiation that occurs, some of the school's most able youngsters complain that they are not being challenged, according to one teacher. Also, the approach may not develop the deep academic background that rigorous thematic, structural, or chronological study can produce.

As a result, students may know a lot about a particular issue or problem in U.S. history but not have a broad overview of events and themes. Furthermore, teachers who share the same students are likely to coordinate instruction, but students are less apt to see connections between what they learn from one grade to the next. It's not unheard of for someone to say she's studied the same theme in U.S. history three times over the past 3 years, for instance.

These would be significant concerns in a Scarsdale, where there is a premium on stretching every student to her fullest, an emphasis on top performance, and less tolerance for loose couplings. In a charter school like High Tech High, parents understand that if they don't like the approach, they don't have to enroll their children. Or, conversely, that if they complain too loudly, the school can suggest they might be happier sending their child elsewhere.

A High Tech High teacher observes that for them, the pluses of the design are worth the sacrifices. Students gain important real-world skills, such as the ability to collaborate, and the level of engagement appears to be high.

BUSINESS LINKS

High Tech High students leave school during all or parts of some days for internships or job-shadowing experiences. The goal is to bridge the gap between academics and the adult world of work. In theory, the connections will help students understand that school learning is meaningful and practically applicable, while preparing them for future careers.

Historically, these kinds of programs have had more mixed results. Students have had to do make-work in menial jobs at their outside placements. Or businesses have found too big a stretch from what youngsters learn in school to what they need to do in a complex, specialized job in the workplace. Or students haven't been available long enough—or they haven't been available at the right times—to make a significant contribution at work.

In addition, only highly evolved businesses have the vision, determination, and resources to take on a task that doesn't improve their quarterly earnings. In the short term, educating young, inexperienced people is a drain of time and money. In the long term, the payoff is uncertain; even when a school is set up to funnel graduates into local jobs, there is no guarantee that they'll stay in the region after they've finished high school and college.

Whatever the difficulties, Riordan says that the school-to-work component of the San Diego program is essential. "It's a connection with the real world. It brings speakers and mentors into the school. Our kids go on visits and internships. And just as important, their teachers go out to visit student workplaces, so they know what's happening in the outplacements, understand expectations in the field, and begin to see ways to connect students' academic work to their experiences in the workplace."

CONNECTIONS

Connection is a recurring theme at High Tech High, reflecting a conscious strategy of helping students understand the meaning and the value of what they're learning. There are connections among academic disciplines; connections among conceptual and hands-on activities, like the Bay Project and model plane construction; connections between the world of school and the world of work. And pupil-teacher relationships are close.

The enrollment of 500 makes it hard for adults to overlook any pupil or for pupils to hide out. Heterogeneous grouping not only diminishes artificial social barriers; it also pushes adults to understand how each student thinks and to treat students individually. When classes are sorted by aptitude into "honors," "regular," and "general" sections, it's easier to teach as if every pupil is the same or similar. To be effective with heterogeneous classes, the instructor has to address individual differences.

The school's project orientation also increases communication. The traditional student–teacher relationship has one kind of dynamic; the relationship with a mentor is different. Further, teachers' real-world backgrounds lend them practical authority: "This is what they do in marine science. Here's how you do what they do."

In addition, common values make connections. Adults and students are to respect one another and to be decent. "We're very clear about drugs, fighting, and respecting the environment," Riordan says. These boundaries, organizational structure, and dependability make productive relationships among adults and youth possible.

In the school's early days, according to Riordan, the naval base was being converted for civilian use and construction surrounded the building. "We made an iron-clad rule that nobody could wander away; if someone got hurt, our whole existence could have been endangered." So, of course, four kids slipped off campus to eat lunch in a partially finished building nearby. "We expelled them," Riordan recalls. "We had to send a message." He pauses and then adds that the four were given a chance to earn readmission—after a semester off.

"Readmission following a semester off" is an important proviso. Effective adult–student connections depend both on fair limits and on students' believing that they are being treated with compassion. In this case, the school sent three important messages: The perpetrators didn't escape responsibility; they had to earn the right to reapply; and they were able to win readmission.

You can sense the results of this hard–soft approach when you walk through the atrium, watch how younger and older people talk with one another, or see how they interact when they're outside at intramurals.

Despite the usual hallway horseplay, the atmosphere is relaxed. Adults offer information and advice, and ask questions without sounding heavy-handed. Kids talk to them informally, often as if they're older peers. But they also listen; the dynamic is purposeful, and work is getting done.

DISCOURSE

Meanwhile, school leaders promote a strong professional culture. A main aim is to develop teaching that responds to students' differences. Riordan says teachers must learn to earn their pupils' trust and to understand how each one thinks. They also have to pick up on signs of understanding, misunderstanding, frustration, discouragement—and then make the right pedagogical moves at the right moment.

This work is the subject of what he calls "the conversation" among professional staff. The premise is that instead of being a place where adults pour information into children's heads, a school is a gathering of people—adults and students—who are all asking and trying to answer important questions. A critical question is how teachers can continue to refine and improve their work. "That's what goes on in a learning community," Riordan says.

At an hour-long meeting each day, faculty discuss, plan, and evaluate programs and instruction, a surprisingly uncommon practice in most schools. For example, the whole staff might examine a piece of student work and discuss what makes it a quality product. The goal of the discussion would be to clarify common expectations and common understandings of what students must do to meet them.

A group of volunteers also might gather weekly to conduct what's called "action research" or "action study" of a current issue. How is one of them teaching a particular lesson? Is it achieving its desired results? Teachers also may meet by academic discipline or in teams (everyone who is involved in the Bay Project, for example). Class observations and visits prompt discourse. Ideas from these smaller conversations may become grist for school-wide discussion.

High Tech High also operates as a graduate school of education that offers a degree-granting master of arts program. As part of their credit-bearing work, a group of teachers may identify an idea and put it into practice. Then they come back, evaluate, and discuss what happened. For example, they might videotape their classes and analyze them in groups of four, perhaps focusing on the way students responded to specific teacher actions. "We used to say our work was 20% theoretical and 80% practical," Riordan comments. "Now we say it's 100% theory embedded in practice."

THE EMPEROR OF RIGOR

Sixty-ish and spare, Riordan left eastern grime and the sleet of Massachusetts in the 1990s to come to California. In Cambridge, he'd helped decentralize the high school, developed award-winning writing programs, and created a model school-to-work initiative. Along the way, he also taught classes at the Harvard Graduate School of Education.

Technically speaking, he became the dean of the school of education at High Tech High, but "what I really am is a critical friend to the school," he observes. "I also see myself as the custodian of the vision." His informal title—Emperor of Rigor—"is a joke, but many people don't get it." He says the "Emperor" part is humorous "because we're not hierarchical. Lots of what we do is done by teams of teachers."

The "Rigor" part has less to do with the difficulty of the academic content and more with helping faculty hold themselves accountable for the longer-term and moment-to-moment decisions they make as they work with students. Videotapes allow them to follow classroom interactions closely (What were you thinking when you spoke to Pedro right then? Why did you intervene there?).

Rigor also implies quality control for the design and assessment of programs and student performance. It has relatively little to do with test scores. Instead, an evaluation of student work might be an exhibition of a product like the books on San Diego Bay, assessed and scored according to rubrics developed by the staff. Possibly, the authors would have to explain their efforts to a panel of adults and defend their findings in a question–answer format.

NATIONAL MODELS

High Tech High School's corporate founders wanted to create a model for urban education. During the October week I visited, the visitors' book at the front desk contained signatures from New York, Chicago, Hawaii, and the Netherlands. But the reason the school draws attention is not because it's a corporate reform showcase. In fact, it doesn't even employ radically new programs or methods.

Some of the school's approaches harken back to the progressive movement of the 1920s. Under the Scarsdale contract plan that I mentioned in Chapter 2, for example, each student had a series of four-week contracts that spelled out the content to be covered each month. Classes met formally either three or four times a week for 60 minutes of discussion or individual study, with students expected to pursue projects and other long-term assignments both in and out of class.

Forty-odd years later, Rabun County High School in Georgia and Kennebunk High School in Maine began to publish *Foxfire* and *Salt* magazines, which featured stories and student research on life and work in communities in the rural South and coastal New England. In the 1970s, Joseph Renzulli, head of the National Research Center on the Gifted and Talented, was encouraging "interested and able" students to identify and study areas of personal interest—to tackle a community problem like wildlife preservation, for instance, and ultimately to present proposed solutions for local officials to address.

School-to-work initiatives also generated interest in the 1970s, when the National Panel on High School and Adolescence (1974) recommended what truly *would* have been revolutionary change. In an earlier era, the panel said, elders had initiated adolescents into the adult world. Now, teenagers were shut off with one another in high schools, where they served time and marked the passage into adulthood with trivial, sometimes dysfunctional, rituals: getting a driver's license, drinking, using drugs.

According to the report, traditional comprehensive high schools were struggling in an uphill effort to educate an increasingly diverse population and to fill a growing number of roles. These "oversized" institutions were increasingly difficult to manage, were artificially held to narrow pedagogical practices, were overburdened with custodial responsibility, and were isolated from the community.

In response, the panel proposed that high schools teach only English, math, science, and social sciences in a dramatically shortened school day. Independent school–community collaborations would then educate students in the arts, government, and careers. Vocational classes would be coordinated with federally funded manpower training programs, community-based work experiences, on-the-job training, career counseling, and job-finding resources.

Like other significant departures from orthodoxy, the panel's report was buried. It may have been vulnerable mostly because of its unsettling proposal to release teens from school custody during the day and give them freedom to move about in their local communities. Nonetheless, limited versions of the school-to-work concept did gain some traction.

At any rate, High Tech High isn't noteworthy because it's a poster child for corporate-style metrics and accountability. Neither are its methods highly original. It is special because it concentrates so intentionally on developing core competencies like critical thinking, because it insists that students show evidence of their competence, and because it does what it does very well: give a highly diverse urban population a quality education.

Like other strong schools, High Tech High has stable governance and leadership with vision. Well-qualified, skilled teachers share the vision and uphold high standards. Parents and students believe in the school and support it. But these strengths didn't materialize out of thin air; they're the result of a strong professional culture, faculty development, and parent involvement.

Administrators and faculty, students, and their parents have built a culture that values learning and promotes thoughtful conversation. That environment generates energy. As Rob Riordan recalls, "I'd go back to Cambridge, and my colleagues would say, 'It's never been worse.'" His shoulders slump and he hangs his head in a mute semblance of weary desperation. "I'd be out here [at High Tech High], and they'd be excitedly asking me to come see what they were doing." School culture, aggressive recruiting, and extensive professional development keep the average level of teaching high. As one staff members says, "What makes the project approach work isn't so much the project approach. It's the teachers." Further, teachers' ongoing interactions ensure that the whole of the faculty is more than the sum of its parts.

Also, parents are invested in their children's education. High Tech High's public exhibitions of student learning grow out of work Riordan and CEO Rosenstock did in Cambridge, where vocational students' parents rarely showed up at traditional back-to-school nights. After a radical curriculum makeover, however, large numbers of parents showed up to see their children demonstrate what they had achieved. The experience convinced the two Massachusetts educators that public exhibitions of learning should be a regular part of life at High Tech High.

So how do High Tech High and schools like Scarsdale compare? In some ways, it's Coke and Pepsi, Yale and Stanford. Scarsdale's graduates gain a perspective that comes from a more classic liberal education. They're academically accomplished, motivated to achieve and to contribute. High Tech High's students present as curious, creative learners. Everyone should hope for the day when differences like these are America's big education concern.

LESSONS FROM CHARTER SCHOOLS

The story of High Tech High is an inspiration to anyone who wants a diverse student population to have a quality education. But the charter movement has to be viewed in a larger context. Charter schools tend to enroll children from upwardly mobile families where parents are engaged and effective advocates. Typically, they can offload difficult students to regular public schools. They also siphon funding from distinct schools and may get preferential treatment when physical space and other resources are being allocated. Private entities often augment their budgets. Also, they are liberated from much of the regular system's regulation and from many of its negotiated work rules.

During the Bloomberg mayoral administration in New York City, for example, it was common to infill one large building with both traditional district and charter schools. With the help of private funds, children in one part of the building could have resources that those in the other part didn't. Advocates of special education programs and parents literally fought City Hall to keep large numbers of children from being placed in buildings where mandated services were provided in locations such as hallways, stairwells, and closets. This kind of disparity has both practical consequences and ethical implications.

What are the logic and equity, furthermore, of granting charter schools regulatory flexibility that those in the district system lack? A High Tech High can hire faculty without meeting the credentialing requirements that apply to district schools, for instance, but in the traditional system, regulations are increasingly rigid. In fact, state education departments actively try to prevent district schools from exercising the creativity that they actively seek to promote in charter education.

For almost 20 years, Ann Cook, head of the New York Performance Standards Consortium and founder of Manhattan's Urban Academy, has waged a dogged fight against state test requirements that are incompatible with the school's project-centered approach to learning. The Academy is a "transfer school" for youngsters who've struggled elsewhere; 52% of its students are economically disadvantaged, according to the New York State Education Department (2013a). The city Department of Education describes it as "Well Developed," meaning that it gets highest grades for highly effective teaching, strategic management, and an excellent learning environment (2013a). Its dropout rate is lower than both city and "peer" school averages, and 90% of graduates go to four-year colleges (Urban Academy, 2013). In contrast, just under 50% of all New York City high school graduates enter two- or four-year college, vocational, or public service programs (New York City Department of Education, 2013b).

In place of high-stakes standardized tests, Consortium schools use projects, experiments, written work, and oral exams to evaluate student progress. High-stakes exams, Cook says, drive curriculum to be broad and shallow, teaching to become narrow and superficial. In contrast, Urban

Academy wants "kids . . . exposed to ideas such as, 'What does this historian think about the reasons for the Civil War? How about that historian?' And then, . . . what do the kids think about the evidence . . . ? Can they present it verbally? Can they argue it out in class? . . . Can they argue it in a written paper? . . . We want a way of teaching that invites and encourages and engages kids to be developing their own point of view and their own perspective based on evidence" (Cook, personal communication, October 14, 2014).

Cook is a bulldog who's pulled few punches in the crusade to preserve her school. In the late 1990s, the State Department of Education tried to force Urban Academy and the other 36 partners in the Standards Consortium to use its tests. Undeterred, Cook, parents, and their allies embarked on a long march of legal action, lobbying, rallies, and media contacts. Through legislative intercession they finally won a reprieve in 2004. A year later, they were back in Albany. Against high odds, they won another victory. Today, despite impressive results, Urban Academy and other schools in the Consortium remain constantly aware of their own vulnerability.

To be sure, semi-independence and regulatory flexibility are not panaceas. While some schools make good use of greater freedom, others require more structured support and regulation. Still, it makes sense to celebrate and encourage places like Urban Academy instead of trying to force them into line. State and federal policy should liberate effective leaders and teachers, as well those who show particular promise, so that they can improve by building on their own strengths.

The rationale for charter schools was that they would do more than educate their own students; they would stimulate innovation and help the much larger traditional system improve. It is time to reflect on how they are carrying out that mission. Should some children be left behind in schools with fewer resources, especially if they are more troubled, lack strong advocates, or have special needs? What should be done to address the shortcomings of a strategy that, in the process of trying to save some youngsters, weakens the system that serves far more? Is the nation best served by policies that balkanize student populations more or less than the current system already does? For charter schooling to be a truly constructive force, America must find better answers to these kinds of questions.

CHAPTER 7

FAITH IN EDUCATION

The phrase "faith in education" evokes memories of efforts to introduce Christian values into the schools of the early 2000s. However, I'm thinking instead about the role belief and leadership play in producing a quality education. I'm also interested in how beliefs shape our reality, often so implicitly that we can't really imagine things being very different from what they are.

I have described America's contradictory beliefs about education. We have praised it as the ladder to success and simultaneously viewed it as inferior to the school of life. We have paid tribute to its value, yet have never been entirely sure about its worth. A subtext is the idea that there's no reason to spend more good money on education than we absolutely have to.

That notion surfaced with a vengeance during the 2008 recession, leading many districts to cut budgets and lay off employees. Scarsdale was fortunate to enter the slowdown on strong financial footing. Few residents wanted to see the schools decimated. Even so, I spent hours talking with taxpayers and exchanging emails about taxes.

Comments fell into a familiar pattern: "Surely, we can cut more money from the budget and not notice the difference." "You should do more with less." "Private sector is reducing headcount; the schools should, too." "Teachers should share residents' sacrifice and give up their salary increases." "Everyone in town knows one or two clunker programs that could be eliminated."

A small, vocal group of the district's critical friends decided to expose what they would likely have described as its financial irresponsibility. The working hypothesis seemed to be that past school boards or administrators, or both, had given away exorbitant increases in teacher salaries and benefits while the public slept. By cutting teachers' pay now, Scarsdale could have it all: a full range of programs and services for much less money.

Our friends' avowed purpose was to serve the public good, but some seemed to see the world almost exclusively through the lens of financial profit and loss; eyes literally rolled heavenward when I tried to explain the educational costs of budget cuts. As one critic said, his goal was to keep education from gobbling up more of his personal resources. He wanted his money in his own pocket.

A handful of residents ventured that the district didn't have to pay highly competitive salaries to attract talented teachers. In fact, they came close to saying that teaching doesn't really have anything to do with learning. The theory was that Scarsdale graduates get into the most selective colleges in the country because their parents went to those schools. Likewise, according to this theory, top SAT scores just reflected good genes, students' work ethic, and outside tutoring. So, according to the line of logic, it should be possible to get the same results for substantially less money.

In reality, families often come to Scarsdale because they see it as a road to colleges the parents didn't attend. Less competitive salaries would affect the quality of the faculty, of teaching, and of graduates' preparation. And that would very likely have an impact on the college admissions some of the disgruntled—at least those with children still in school—very probably do care about. The way to find out would be to test the hypothesis, an experiment a majority of residents probably would prefer not to try.

Anyway, the school board and the teachers' association had already agreed on the need to moderate salary growth. But whatever they did, our friends could outflank them on the Right. Responding to calls for a salary give-back, the union agreed to reduce pay and benefits by $2.1 million, although it had no legal obligation even to discuss the topic in mid-contract.

The fiscal hawks said the board had made a bad deal and should have gotten more.

Certain of the critics described themselves as pragmatists, sincerely concerned about the district's financial health. That was doubtless true for some, but where others were concerned, one sensed the hint of opportunism. They certainly hadn't been at board meetings proposing to invest more when the economic engine was humming.

I don't share these stories just to vent my personal frustrations. The topic of the chapter is belief, and what I've just described is a system of belief and a political context that is so common in America, it's unremarkable. We may not all be fiscal hawks, but we nod reflexively when we hear calls for "hard budget choices" and fiscal sustainability.

In a different reality, paying teachers excellent salaries would be understood to have long-term value, and education wouldn't be seen as a drain on people's income. More people might believe that real financial prudence or a truly hard budget choice could be to invest more in schools. Forget fuzzy notions about learning for self-fulfillment or democracy. Assume that the main purpose of school is to produce workers for a 21st-century economy, as corporate reform proposes.

Self-evidently, teachers who are talented and well educated are more likely to produce well-educated students than those who aren't. In the world's top-performing nations, teachers come from the highest third of their university classes. In America, top college graduates usually don't become schoolteachers. A rational strategy for increasing our economic productivity would be to invest more money in recruiting, educating, and retaining top teaching talent.

Obviously, we do not. The reason isn't that our states or the nation can't. It's that we value other things more and find it hard to think differently about priorities. To be sure, some of us do live in or on the edge of real poverty and truly cannot contribute more. In the past decade, however, we have collectively spent billions on homeland security and overseas wars. Our prison population is a quarter of the world's total, and each prisoner costs about $27,000 a year (Schmitt, Warner, & Gupta, 2010). As individuals, we spend huge amounts on fashionable basketball shoes, cigarettes, alcohol, cars, and pickups that gulp gasoline. Those are choices, not immutable facts. The fiscal hawks say the trajectory of school budgets is unsustainable. In fact, the public decides what's sustainable by deciding what it's willing to pay for.

WHAT HAPPENED TO FAITH IN PUBLIC EDUCATION?

Thomas Jefferson was right. For much of our history, most Americans needed only a simple education, one that was also relatively inexpensive. Schools were largely under local control and relatively responsive to local residents. Few people even thought about the condition of public education at large. Faith in the system somehow rose above their frustrations with it.

Today, many Americans believe that the system is failing. Why? Part of the answer has to do with demographics and rising expectations. In the early 1900s, only about 10% of high school–age youth were in school, and fewer graduated. By 1945, about 40% left with a diploma. In the year 2000, almost everyone was in school until at least age 16 (Ravitch, 1983). The schools were expected to educate them all while also meeting higher standards and addressing a broader array of social problems.

Americans could have understood this story as a tale of achievement and continuing challenge, but the rising bar made the schools look worse than before. In addition, urbanization and the industrial model of education had led to school district consolidation and larger schools. Bigger may have been better in financial terms, but size also had costs.

Historically, elected boards of education straddled the boundary be-tween school and community, interpreting one to the other. In the 1930s, there were more than 200,000 boards of education in the United States. Only 15,000 survived in 2000, serving well over twice the number of people (Meier, 2003). Necessarily, a smaller percentage of adults knew the people on their boards—assuming they had elected boards at all.

The average citizen also was less likely to know a student or a teacher, or to be invested in his or her own child's education. In 1900, almost 40% of the population was of school age; by the 1990s, it had fallen below 20% (Snyder, 1993). The percent of people who were teachers was also smaller. In addition, more of the young were poor and minorities. As far as some Americans were concerned, these "other" children were some-body else's problem.

In short, large numbers of citizens had less opportunity or reason to understand educators, schools, or the young people in them. Therefore, it shouldn't be a surprise that only about 40% of adults without children gave their local schools good marks in the 2000s. Or that both they, and parents as well, held negative attitudes toward public education in gen-eral (Rose & Gallup, 2004).

Into this void stepped the business community, politicians, and the media. Public education was a far-flung, diverse enterprise with high highs, low lows, and a lot in between. The gap between economic and ethnic groups was persistent and widespread, but some schools did a good job of serving poor children and children of color. Still, the newspapers and TV had little incentive to explore these complexities. The narrative of mass systems failure was simple and perversely self-justifying.

By definition, news was eye-catching, unsettling, and bizarre. Up front were school shootings and victimized children, Christian values and evolution, budgets and financial skullduggery, political conflict, sta-tistically meaningless test score comparisons, and school rankings. More meaningful stories were apt to be buried somewhere on page 30, if they were printed at all.

Also, education reporting was a journalistic backwater. Usually, those who got marooned there weren't trained social scientists or knowledge-able about education, and they often didn't know what questions to ask. A surprising number of editorial boards and columnists seemed remark-ably incurious about flaws in the corporate narrative, which they contin-ued to write about uncritically.

As the news business became more straitened, coverage often be-came even more superficial. Following a weekend drinking party in Scarsdale, for example, area TV cameramen camped out across from the high school, where they took pictures of the football team walking out to practice. Advocacy "news" and the blogosphere presented an increasingly distorted picture of reality, even as the 24-hour cycle invited over-simplification and caricature.

News and feature pieces described test score scandals or "revolutionary" ideas about schooling ("What If the Secret to Success Is Failure?" asked a 2011 *New York Times* magazine piece). Collectively, as I said earlier, the media continued to promote the idea that America had "a school problem," as if all the districts in the country shared the same difficulty. Presumably, this problem demanded simple answers: Force the education establishment to do its job; create competition. Nobody else needed to exert more effort or make any kind of sacrifice.

Corporate reform advocates wanted to institutionalize these beliefs. The media amplified their message and simultaneously undermined faith in the idea of public education itself. Given the impressive array of businesses, government, and media people promoting the narrative, it was surprising that Americans had as much faith in the schools as they did.

WHY BELIEF MATTERS

Whatever was happening on a larger scale, meanwhile, local confidence in local schools could be persistent. In 2013, their parent approval rating was 71% (Bushaw & Lopez, 2013). In places like Scarsdale, families paid high housing prices and taxes, largely because they believed they were putting their children on track to college and a good life.

For generations, a majority of Scarsdale residents had invested in teachers because they believed that would help children achieve. Strong teachers motivated children. Invested parents, strong teaching, and motivated children attracted new families who shared the same beliefs. The self-reinforcing cycle of faith lifted the schools above their critics.

These values correlated with a belief in achievement, whether on the playing field or stage or in the classroom—ideally, in all three. Kids in the high school sat on hallway floors, backs propped against the wall, actually studying or reading for class. Some who would have been on the margins in other places were respected because they were good at math or accomplished in the speech contest. As one high school freshman said at an orientation meeting, it was cool to be smart.

Belief also caused teachers to work long hours and to invest themselves in their students. In my first year as superintendent, I suggested hiring a new teacher specifically to help special-needs students who might have trouble passing state tests. One of the regular teachers took umbrage. That was *her* job, she said; those were her kids, and she was responsible for doing what it took for them to succeed.

To be certain, the culture had downsides, including significant pressure to succeed and a belief that good grades and success were one and the same. Recent graduates commented that high school was more difficult than their first year at college. Some said that their focus on college admission had kept them from pursuing other rewarding options. Also, places like Scarsdale could be difficult if you really cut across the grain—if you didn't buy into life on the fast track, for example.

Scarsdale isn't unique. In an earlier life, I was head of a prominent independent school. Before I went there, I'd always assumed that places like it succeeded because they accepted smart kids, then got rid of any problem students who somehow slipped through the screening process. I thought they didn't admit bad apples, or threw them out so only good ones were left.

It turned out that the students weren't all brilliant, and they had their share of problems and insecurities. Having been raised with much less privilege, I found some of their trials a bit otherworldly: the trauma of being accepted at Yale and Princeton but denied at Harvard, for example. Still, some of them had messy home situations, serious personal difficulties, and other problems I might not have expected in "a place like that."

I also learned that the school's strength derived from its powerful core values. A common belief in the importance of achievement pushed students to do well. Some of the school's authority came from the fact that it *could* let students go, not that it did; we dismissed fewer than a handful while I was there. As in Scarsdale, both school and family committed themselves to make the most of the apples they had. A quality education was the result.

WHEN BELIEF EBBS

My first administrative job was in a very different world. In the early 1970s, I worked in a struggling New Hampshire mill town that was as reminiscent of Appalachia as of the urban Northeast. Project Follow Through, which I headed, was a federal anti-poverty, K–3 education program. It was one of 178 such locations nationwide. The different projects were supposed to determine which of several educational models was most likely to help poor children.

The name of our model was the Open Classroom. It promoted positive self-image and featured rooms with learning centers, where the child's interests were supposed to determine her activities. Although our own students made learning gains, the results of the Open Classroom more generally were unimpressive. It turned out that positive self-image without skills was not an education, and the best way to get young people to learn basic skills was by teaching them basic skills.

Our program's success was likely due to several factors. Although they weren't supposed to, technically speaking, teachers modified the model, pragmatically combining student-initiated learning with skills-directed teaching. They also had rich professional development opportunities. In addition, staff helped parents solve the challenges of hardscrabble lives and enabled them to support their children's learning. For example, out-reach workers taught parents how to help their children use educational toys borrowed from a toy library.

At least as important, children were reasonably well fed and healthy, a result both of federal assistance and of an independent well-child clin-ic established by Follow Through social workers. Like James Comer's (2009) later efforts in New Haven and the Children's Zone in Harlem, the program reached out into the community and provided students with wraparound services. Parents worked as teacher aides and studied for as-sociate's degrees through college extension courses.

My New Hampshire memories sometimes haunt me. I think about one of our parents, Annie Prevost (a pseudonym). Annie's solid body held her to the ground, but she exuded a sort of magnetism. She smoked more or less constantly. While you couldn't ignore the emptiness where her teeth were missing, the arresting angles of her face and her brilliant blue eyes told you that in a different life she would have been stunning.

Annie had several children and a drinking problem, and men drifted in and out of her life. Her apartment on the third floor of a gray clapboard double-decker had been built for mill workers years ago. Now listing slightly westward, it overlooked a poorly paved street that ultimately dwindled into wilderness. Annie was probably about my age, in her late 20s or early 30s.

Two of her children were in the primary grades and ate breakfast daily at school. One was a biter. Other parents worried about his being in class with their children. Both boys were easily distracted, neither able to focus for more than a few minutes at a time; today, we might find that they had attention deficit disorder.

When she felt like it, Annie would come over to the parent center, two doors down from her building. There we'd talk. I'd urge her to get into the extension program. She would listen patiently, smile winningly, and agree with me. We'd discuss how she had to get a job, which some-times seemed about to happen, but for the regular accidents in her life. She'd appear with bruises and a black eye. Or a boyfriend would show up and she'd disappear.

At some point, I realized that nothing was going to change. Her life was about lack of structure. Despite her native intelligence, I don't think she had the experience, understanding, or determination—or perhaps any of the three—to live any differently.

These memories connect me to an interim superintendent in southern Alaska. Here's what she told me.

Miles apart from one another, the four schools in her former district serve a total of 400 students, about half Native American. Attendance is poor, graduations minimal, college out of the picture. Anyone with academic or professional ambitions goes to a government-sponsored boarding school hundreds of miles away.

When he's not in school, the superintendent says, a typical Native American teenager wakes up late, talks on the cell phone, plays video games, watches TV. Social life is about drinking and casual sex, some combination of which may last late into the night. Alcoholism and teen pregnancy are widespread. Newborns often have fetal alcohol syndrome.

Students are friendly and generally compliant in class, but they are also listless and uninvolved. Teachers are mostly well meaning, not well trained, and no match for the challenges they face. Turnover is high. The newest faculty member in one building has been there 7 months. She'll probably leave at the end of the year.

As recently as 50 years ago, many Native people led spare but purposeful lives in accordance with traditional ways. They hunted, fished, dried food, made clothing, cared for children and one another. The culture centered on subsistence values: cooperating, maintaining relationships, loving children, accepting hard reality. The values endure, but they have little to do with the kind of academic learning that is supposed to prepare people for living in a global community. According to the superintendent from Alaska, the loss of the old ways and their children's lack of direction dismay parents, but they see no alternatives. They lack the kind of education that would allow them to support formal schooling in the home. They accept and sometimes enable their children's behavior, seeing White intrusion as the source of their problems, distrusting the government and others who have visited alien ways on them.

Outsiders may or may not be out to exploit them, but these people are the prey of an invading culture. They live on the verge of spiritual and, in some cases, literal suicide. What the rest of America apparently has to offer them is the shallowest Western materialism and its hollow gratifications: cell phones, TV, substance abuse.

In the early 2000s, the corporate reform agenda mainly seemed to suggest that the answer to the problems in places like Alaska—or Detroit—was higher standards, more tests, and greater accountability, surely a useful prescription for people in devastation. Later, it prescribed school choice, closing failing schools, firing incompetent teachers, a better quality of testing, and teacher ratings—also productive strategies.

FOSTERING BELIEF

I have tried to think about how I would salvage the seemingly hopeless situation in Alaska. In a better world, I would bring in highly skilled teachers. I'd give them opportunities for professional development. I'd try to meet the Native students in intellectual territory they might find meaningful and interesting. Beginning with whatever ideas or information would engage them, I could try to connect what they knew with significant content in history, literature, and science.

I would consider using computer technology and High Tech High–style projects. I'd try to connect school and real-world learning. Students could be involved in team-building, mentored by respected adults. There'd be better outreach to the home: better health and nutrition services and support for parents, so they could help their children in school.

However, even if I could find highly qualified teachers willing to live a 6-hour boat ride from Juneau, and even if there were money for these efforts, my ideas might be completely irrelevant. Native American kids might never see value in discussions about ideas I think are important. I might not win their trust or cooperation.

So maybe a different strategy would be better. Native peoples around the world are trying to gain control of their lives, partly by building their own forms of education. Could local residents of isolated spots in Alaska use that approach to create school communities that involve students, parents, and village leaders? I don't know.

Whatever the answer, I do know that little will change until the children and their families come to believe that formal education has some meaning. What the young learn has to connect with what they value, and it must give them a sense of efficacy. Otherwise, the next generation is lost. The same could be said of children in other struggling communities across the United States.

BELIEF AND LEADERSHIP

A successful education depends on faith. People invest themselves and their resources in things they believe in: Alumni give to the annual fund not because their college is number 1 in the *U.S. News* rankings but because the college experience changed their lives. America's public schools suffer for lack of similar commitment.

That is why the most basic challenge of public school leadership is to articulate a vision of a quality education, to galvanize belief in that idea, and then to channel human energy in pursuit of it. The work is difficult for many reasons, but especially because it asks people to transcend a reality they know and beliefs they already have.

I recently met a young mom who can't understand why Scarsdale teachers have to take so many inservice courses that raise her taxes. A main reason she moved to town was to get her daughter a credential that will get her into a good college. She grew up in the rust belt and didn't go to schools like her child's; even though she may understand the function of professional development intellectually, her life experience doesn't dispose her to value it. So she does not support it.

Why is this story important? The quality of public education depends on popular consensus, which in turn reflects people's beliefs. (The schools will only provide robust professional development opportunities if enough voters value the activity, for example.) Normally, that consensus rides on conventional wisdom and momentum: what has been tends to determine what is and will be. But critics are always pulling away at the fabric of the institution, and their voices grow stronger in hard economic times.

Just to maintain a school or district's existing quality, therefore, leaders have to continually educate community members about what is valuable and why. Getting residents to support change can be an even bigger challenge, especially if it means asking them to transcend what they know and are comfortable doing. (In the case of the young mom, for instance, to value an activity she has no great disposition to value: staff development.) Where does that kind of leadership come from? What does it look like?

Thomas Sobol, former commissioner of education in New York State, is the son of a Boston brewery worker. He won admission to the selective public Boston Latin School, went to Harvard, and served in the Army.

Former U.S. secretary of education Rod Paige is the son of a school principal and a teacher. An African American born in heavily segregated Monticello, Mississippi, he worked his way through Jackson State University, where he quarterbacked the football team.

Originally a teacher of English and later school superintendent in Scarsdale, Sobol became New York State's chief education officer in 1987. A gifted advocate for public schooling, he described the urgency of providing all children the education that is their birthright. Schools must "give them the skills and discipline and love they need to feel good about themselves and to become constructive members of society," he said (Carmody, 1987).

During his 9 years in Albany, Sobol introduced a comprehensive policy initiative that sought to provide "top-down support for bottom-up reform." It called on all partners in the education enterprise—communities, parents, students, schools, the state—to become mutually accountable for improving student learning. The plan focused on assessment, teaching quality, sound curriculum, and parent involvement. It assumed there were no quick or simple fixes.

Especially in a populous and diverse state like New York, broad, meaningful school improvement was always going to take time. The window of opportunity was narrow when Sobol took office; state politics and the State Education Department bureaucracy had always been more about top-down mandates than about deep, reflective change. As the corporate agenda gained momentum, furthermore, the ineluctable logic of metrics and the prevailing political winds started to point down the narrower path of education by the numbers.

Sobol resigned in 1996. Under his successor, Richard Mills, SED began to focus "like a laser" on test score improvement. Officials heralded the annual arrival of state "report cards" on student performance. More students took more tests. Accountability was the watchword. Realizing that their role was to do the state's bidding, many front-line educators submitted quietly and tried to keep a low profile.

About the same time, having coached college football and led the education department at Texas Southern University, Rod Paige was elected to the school board in Houston, TX. Then, in 1994, amid heavy politicking and bitter infighting, he was named superintendent of schools there. Over the next 6 years, he attracted widespread attention for engineering a corporate-style district turnaround.

Despite the stresses surrounding his appointment, Paige was a popular school leader, especially in the business community. In close collaboration with corporate and community advisers, the Houston Independent School District devolved decisionmaking to the school level, emphasizing principals' accountability for test and graduation results. Paige introduced performance contracts and incentive pay for principals, and he promoted charter schools. Test scores improved.

After Paige was named U.S. Secretary of Education in 2000, newspapers began to report that Houston's graduation rates and scores had been artificially inflated (FairTest, 2004; Leung, 2004). Administrators had found ways to hide or avoid reporting poor results. District employees also said that the rapid reforms had confused and demoralized staff at least as much as they had helped improve the schools. In Washington, Paige claimed these controversies were local matters and no longer his concern. He resigned from the national post in 2005.

The common themes in these two men's stories are their hardscrabble childhoods, self-reliance, and public schooling. The difference is that Sobol's experience gave him faith in the system; in a Scarsdale graduation speech, he described his public education as the reason he'd been able to transcend the numbing conditions of his early life. In Paige's world, the system couldn't be trusted. He once said he was a Republican because when he was young, the Democrats were the ones who were trying to lynch you (Winters, 2001).

Paige may be remembered best for calling the National Education Association a "terrorist organization" (Pear, 2004) and for saying that if he'd had the choice, he'd have sent his children to schools that taught Christian values (Schemo, 2003). He explained by saying he was simply acknowledging that private schools have clear, shared goals, while public schools do not because they serve so many diverse students with diverse values. Whatever he did mean, it sounded very much as if the nation's chief public school officer didn't support public education.

Paige may not have intended his comment the way it came out. If he did realize how it would be heard, maybe he was responding to a right-wing political base. Or maybe he was trying to shape public opinion to support a deregulated school marketplace that would operate on business principles and reflect conservative Christian values.

Regardless, the statement was significant because of its implicit premise: Public schools do an inferior job of teaching children to become Americans. Considering the role of public education in Paige's own life, it was especially ironic and poignant.

Paige could have invoked a sense of national purpose. He could have said that for all its shortcomings, public education has brought a diverse people together, provided us a shared narrative, helped us to live and work together, or given many of us better lives. He could have said that public schools deserve public support because they're essential to our collective future and need our help now. That's not what he did.

Tom Sobol had the vision and the rhetorical power to ignite commitment to the promise of public education. When the way forward is unclear, that's what great leaders do. They offer a new way to understand the world, one that resonates with people's most basic beliefs. The people see how this way of thinking leads to a better future. They gather around the vision. That changes the social and political dynamic, and the impossible becomes doable.

The 2010 movie *Waiting for "Superman"* (Chilcott & Guggenheim) promoted the idea that no superhero is coming to save the children in America's crumbling public education system, so it is up to regular people to rescue them by supporting reforms like charter schools. The film was off-target in many respects, but its premise was correct: Superman is not going to drop by.

If we want our nation to be great tomorrow, we must reach within, summon up our powers, and give every American child a great education. We can find consensus on the value and purposes of our public schools. We can disavow the corporate reform's distorted vision and reaffirm the value of an education for democracy. We can disregard the misuses of metrics, and we can honor meaningful teaching and learning. We, the people, can transform our schools and our nation.

CHAPTER 8

EDUCATION FOR DEMOCRACY

If you don't know where you are going, it is hard to get there. And the objective of public education can range from liberating talent to preparing efficient workers to getting good test scores to producing good linebackers, depending on who you happen to be talking with. Consensus being unlikely, communities often adopt generic mission statements that espouse unarguable goals. Thereafter, the schools respond pragmatically to educational and political forces that arise in the normal course. How can an education be good, let alone great, if people don't know or disagree about what it is supposed to achieve?

Public school governance is the responsibility of officials who either are elected or appointed by people who are elected. Their decisions necessarily reflect political considerations as well as educational merit. School priorities also depend on state regulations and labor contracts. Faculties may believe that their academic authority should guide educational choices. At least some residents are apt to think business principles should.

In the last half of the 20th century, accordingly, the real—as distinct from the stated—mission of public schools grew more complex and diffuse. New programs and services addressed changing college and career expectations. New laws dramatically expanded students' rights and required schools to add women's athletic teams to comply with Title IX. Extensive new special education divisions came into being. A variety of new "educations" dealt with controversial issues from sex to drugs to prejudice to bullying.

All these programs and services were worthwhile, but how many things could one institution do well? Districts had to be careful about spreading their energies thin and diluting their quality in the best of times. When the economy weakened, popular programs competed with ones that had more academic value. The results could be troubling. Financial cost being equal, for instance, what was likely to survive: teachers' professional development, a well-attended teen center, or varsity football?

An unclear mission also made it inevitable that constituencies would work at cross-purposes, often failing to see that their problem was a difference in goals. Consider, for instance, the ongoing debate about teaching evolution. Underlying arguments over the merits of creationism (or "intelligent design") and science were questions of mission: Is education a process of inquiry or of inculcating faith?

MISSION: ELIMINATING AP

Remember Scarsdale's 2001 state testing controversy? Should education be a competition for high test scores or an experience that leads to deep understanding? The confrontation between district and state consumed local officials, teachers, and parents as they debated issues, communicated with Albany, and managed media contacts. In the process, teaching and learning took a backseat.

Five years later, Scarsdale was in the middle of another dispute that was basically about its mission. After 2 years of research, the high school faculty had voted to replace Advanced Placement (AP) classes with courses called advanced topics (AT). If the Board of Education agreed, Scarsdale High School would be the first public school in the United States to drop the AP program.

The purpose of AP was to allow high school students to do accelerated work that would earn credit once they got to college. The College Board, which sponsored AP, didn't provide written curriculums for its courses. The program consisted solely of academic subject tests developed by university professors and schoolteachers. In practice, however, the content of the tests defined *de facto* what teachers taught.

Over the years, AP had become the nation's academic gold standard. Participation swelled from just over 177,000 students in 1983 (the year of ANAR) to 1.8 million in 2010 (College Board, 2010). More students had access to higher-quality curriculums, but the rapid growth also raised questions about equity and excellence. How many more people could reasonably be expected to meet a very high standard, and at what point would the tests have to be watered down?

There were also concerns about the integrity of AP instruction. Teachers had gotten very good at gaming the exams. They knew the point value of each section, the number of points required for a satisfactory score in each, and the content that was likely to be tested. Calculating the most likely routes to success, they prepped their students strategically for the exams. Some even talked with pride about "their" AP results. Students might get good scores, but what did they have to do with real learning?

Theoretically, the AP program gave teachers considerable latitude to teach what was important and interesting. In practice, it offered relatively little. Especially in courses like biology and U.S. history, the tests covered an overwhelming amount of detailed content. Students spent the year trying to study it all and prepping for everything that might be tested. There was little time to follow individual interests or to explore other topics in depth.

AP tests didn't necessarily align with university requirements, either. They could be slow to adapt to emerging trends, and the 2- or 3-hour exam format didn't accommodate extended research, longer papers, and other work that colleges valued. More class time for these activities meant less time to learn things that might be tested, which meant that scores could suffer. Additionally, some Scarsdale teachers objected to the cynical business of coaching students to amass the right number of points so they could get a "passing" score of 3 or better.

The faculty thought about these issues and proposed their alternative program in response. Teachers would begin to replace "mile-wide, inch-deep" curriculums with more in-depth instruction. Courses would evolve more nimbly in response to college expectations, as well as student and faculty interests. If they wanted college credit, students would still be able to take AP exams; AT courses just wouldn't focus on them.

The one metric that mattered most in Scarsdale was college acceptance, so the high school guidance department surveyed the 100 colleges and universities most graduates attended. Overwhelmingly, the message was that as long as Scarsdale clearly identified college-level courses on students' transcripts, their label didn't matter. Harvard and the University of Pennsylvania actively encouraged the transition.

In the fall of 2006, nonetheless, you might well have attended a parent–teacher meeting and heard a mother worrying about her son's admission chances if he lacked an "AP" label on his transcript. Surely, the guidance department must be overselling the colleges' assurances. Why couldn't the faculty just teach what they wanted and keep the label? Why diverge from the AP gold standard in the first place?

"Let's say we're discussing Jefferson and Hamilton," the teacher might say. "Populism and less government, elitism and activist government. The class is really cooking, and I want to connect the history to current events. That'll take me a few more days, which I could manage by cutting time off from teaching the War of 1812 and the Mexican–American War. But I worry I might not cover something that will be on the AP test. So I play it safe and move on. The kids lose."

"But the test guarantees that you'll teach the right content. Why can't you do that and also cover what *you* want to, as well?" the parent might counter.

"There just isn't enough time to go over all the detail that could be on the test and also to explore how the Jefferson and Hamilton conflict applies today. But you know Scarsdale teachers. Wouldn't you trust us to adjust the curriculum?"

"I'd trust *you*," she says, "but who knows who the teacher will be next year, when my son is a senior?"

Part of the difference here is a basic difference in assumptions. In the parent's view, AP U.S. history is an important body of knowledge that's defined by "expert historians." Scarsdale teachers may be well meaning, but their job is to deliver the content. The all-important test certifies that they've done their job. In the teacher's view, history can be understood in many ways. His job is to help students make sense of evidence that is often equivocal. The AP test is one way to evaluate their efforts, but it's not necessarily the best.

To complicate matters, the parent's explicit concerns may not be the only issues. As I've said, many people move to places like Scarsdale assuming they've entered into a tacit compact: "You have my moral and financial support; get my daughter into a good college and on her way to the good life." The faculty's AT proposal seems to threaten this covenant. There is no guarantee that their unproven scheme will achieve what the parent may well see as the school's primary mission: putting her child on track for the future.

Between September and November 2006, the high school principal and teachers talk with more parents. Exchanges become more contentious. "AP sets a standard everyone understands. Why fix what's not broken?" "No matter what anyone says, colleges are less likely to accept kids without AP." "Teachers are trying to make their lives easier and avoid accountability." "If my daughter can't earn AP credit in high school, she won't be able to opt out of courses at university." "The College Board says AP lets teachers teach what and how they want, so what's the problem?"

All the issues are specific, but the underlying differences are about mission. As I reflect on this idea, I flash back to a recent email exchange with the president of my undergraduate college. I'd suggested they consider adding some education courses, pointing out how I thought that would further the college's mission. "Thanks," he wrote back, slightly more politely than this, "but no thanks. We know what we're doing. We define the mission and we have the authority to carry it out. You don't."

My world is very different. Anyone in town can weigh in on the schools' direction, and it sometimes feels as if everyone wants to. Normally, the utilitarian goal of getting kids into college doesn't seem to be at odds with the academic goal of providing them a deep, rich education. But now, some parents think the AT plan threatens their children's college and life chances. Teachers believe it will do a better job of getting them to think well, which also will prepare them better for college.

It's November 2006. Whatever the district's mission is on paper, its real mission is in dispute. The faculty have endorsed the AT proposal. Some parents have voiced support. A more vocal group actively opposes the idea. A large number (whose children aren't about to take either AP or AT courses) are waiting to see what happens.

MISSION AND BOARD STEWARDSHIP

Residents let board members know their views at meetings and in the other usual ways: at social events, through emails, over the supermarket counter. The board says it supports the proposal in concept, but is listening to the community and will outline a plan to review the topic. It hosts public meetings that sometimes bring teachers and parents together, sometimes feature direct trustee exchanges with parents.

These encounters are mostly civil. In one, however, a frustrated teacher tells parents flatly they should trust the faculty and stop trying to micromanage the schools. She's invoking an academic model of governance, where the experts make decisions on issues within their competence. Some parents are equally blunt in expressing their opposition. They believe they are living in a democracy, where constituents influence their representatives to make decisions that they support.

By the following spring, everything that possibly could be said about the issues has been said—many times. Some compromises are possible. The plan can be phased in and monitored; it can include quality controls—curriculum reviews by university scholars and program reviews by teacher–parent committees. The school can prep students outside of class if they want to take AP tests.

In the end, however, people simply have different ideas about priorities. After months of discussion, the board hosts the last of several public forums. The president outlines a format for the evening. About 5 minutes into the meeting, though, a father objects that the board is being unresponsive. Despite all the research and discussion, he says, this radical new idea is moving too quickly. The board should slow down and consider it in some possible future. "What's the hurry?" he asks, rhetorically. He's on the verge of abandoning representative government for pure democracy.

Depending on what happens next, the entire situation could disintegrate. The district could be consigned to months of confrontation involving board members, professional staff, and parents. More likely, the discussion will subside wearily into stalemate. If that happens, the faculty, who have been enthusiastic about a new and better program, will be demoralized and cynical.

The board president listens carefully, then acknowledges the speaker's point. Smiling, she says again that the trustees have agreed tentatively to proceed with the AT plan, but it must be well considered and address parent concerns. In the charged atmosphere of the packed meeting, she has just clarified that the district's mission isn't decided by plebiscite on a specific issue.

The board is more than a group of representatives. The public has entrusted it and each of its members to act as stewards of the institution. On behalf of the citizens, they are to exercise their own, more-informed judgment about what measures are in students' best interest. Consistent with the mission and broad community values, they decide which programs may go forward.

In June, the board approves an AT Phase One for the following fall. Every critic isn't convinced. Still, this is a community where most people are civil and respect open process. The board's tradition of openness and the trustees' personal credibility earn public confidence. The board's judgment will be honored.

What's the final word on AT? In Scarsdale, one can never be totally sure, but 3 years later, AT classes feature experiences teachers would have been reluctant to include before: original research at the Kennedy and Franklin Roosevelt presidential libraries, for example. Students have more opportunities to examine issues and events from alternative perspectives. There are more connections between academic study and the real world, more simulations, debates, primary-source analyses, outside readings. Teachers say they can respond better to emerging topics and interests.

Eighty-seven percent of students rate AT as "good" to "outstanding" overall, while 85% say the courses are "very good" to "outstanding" at expanding their thinking. Students also rate AT courses more positively than AP courses in terms of stimulating curiosity and love of learning. College admissions results are at least as strong as before, and there has been no identifiable change in the scores of AP test-takers.

Finally, visiting college professors have validated the initiative. One comments, for example, that "it's remarkable how probing and thoughtful the Scarsdale faculty is in asking students to engage in higher level work. . . . [The students] demonstrate many of the skills of my best at Oberlin." After two professors describe changes they're introducing at Cornell, Scarsdale's science chair expresses thanks for the way "they encouraged us to recognize that not everything in the text is important. They said universities are giving us permission to change along with them."

From the superintendent's perspective, this certainly sounds encouraging. Nonetheless, consider the time and energy invested in a political process that related only indirectly to teaching and learning. Then think about how the issue might have played out if the community had less underlying confidence in the schools, if the board were more distant from the people, or if the trustees had been more fearful of dissent or interested in avoiding controversy—as is so often the case.

MISSION AND DIVERSITY

Public education is rooted in the soil of small towns and midsize communities like Scarsdale, where personal relations, local organizations, and volunteer activities tend to perpetuate comity and confidence in elected officials. Even under the best of conditions, however, problems of mission interfere with efforts to improve teaching and learning.

Still, as the AT experience illustrates, strong leadership and consensus-building can advance education quality in an environment of controlled conflict. Officials took principled positions and responded to community views by creating oversight committees and the visiting professor plan. The public process was messy, time-consuming, and sometimes unpleasant. But this "inefficient" approach to a problem of mission helped residents sort out the issues and end up "owning" a workable outcome.

Ideally, the democratic process would enable all school communities to embrace a collective mission and piece together enough common ground to move forward. But in a socially and politically fragmented nation where impatience with authority is widespread, how much common ground can there be? How many Americans have the patience to tolerate their differences and to give democracy time to work?

Especially in communities that are both large and diverse, relatively few personal relationships, traditions, or formal social structures hold the whole together. Different interests can obscure institutional mission, divert energy from efforts to achieve it, even erupt into open conflict. A traditional way of managing this problem has been to centralize authority in a large bureaucracy. More recent has been the trend toward radical decentralization, which is evident in the charter school movement.

In a large centralized bureaucracy, those with formal authority determine the mission, while rules and regulations insulate decisionmakers from special interests and self-interest. This kind of structure worked during New York City's "golden age" of education in the early and mid-20th century, largely because many children came from striving families that valued formal learning. The achievers flourished; others weren't expected to meet high standards. Overall, the results were impressive for the time, even though they were uneven.

The obvious weakness of a large system is the ease with which it can become pervasively unresponsive. When leadership is distant from the grass roots and a large middle bureaucracy is insulated from account-ability, relationships among the system's parts—central authority, schools, teachers, parents—grow more attenuated. In that event, collaboration be-tween the parts is less probable, conflict more likely.

Alternatively, the decentralization and selectivity of charter schools—their ability to admit or dismiss students—increases the likelihood of a clear sense of mission. Clear mission, along with a motivated, upwardly mobile clientele, is a real advantage. But as I noted in Chapter 6, the char-ter movement is not without its drawbacks either.

What, if any, other alternatives are there?

FORGING COMMON MISSION

The quality of governance is critical to mission-driven leadership. Yet peo-ple get on boards of education for many reasons: to save money, to oust the superintendent, to promote the football program, or to get in line for higher office, among others. In addition, board dynamics are complicated; personal frictions are reasonably common, for example.

Some places respond by inventing structures whose objective is to minimize dysfunction and promote effective leadership. For example, Scarsdale in the progressive 1920s developed a nonpartisan system for identifying school board candidates. Over the years, it also established the tradition of limiting board member terms.

Under the nonpartisan system, residents elect a school board nomi-nating committee of citizens. The committee looks for candidates whose only agenda is to listen carefully, to make wise decisions, and to give students a good education within reasonable financial limits. The com-munity's confidence in this process means that elections are usually uncontested.

Trustees do not serve multiple terms, as they do in many other places. The "two-term" tradition protects the system against entrenched "professional" board members whose pursuit of reelection or personal agendas might start to displace interest in the larger public good. The board majority is always experienced; the group is always renewing itself. It has an insider's perspective and one that's relatively close to constituents. Superintendents serve relatively long terms and provide professional continuity.

There is no perfect board member (or superintendent). Trustees' views reflect both the better and the worse impulses of the community and of the broader society. But on balance, the nominating process and term limits have helped to cultivate generations of elected leaders who have broadly represented their fellow residents and who have tried to work as a team.

Over time, and with some exceptions, the board has focused less on mechanics and more on larger questions and strategic goals. Its vision and direction have been unusually consistent. Individual perspectives have differed, but members have listened respectfully to one another, so that their ideas evolved. In the end, despite disagreements, they supported the group's conclusions. There's been a minimum of backdoor politicking.

The structures that have helped Scarsdale focus on a coherent mission might be relevant elsewhere, but they are also place-specific. For instance, they'd be wholly inadequate to the challenges in New York City, where the public schools educate 1.1 million children and where powerful forces pull the institution in many different directions. (In fact, I always wonder what would make a system of 1.1 million of *anything* work at a consistently high level.)

New York City has both a bureaucracy whose leader reports to the mayor and the extreme decentralization of charter schooling. Given the limitations of both approaches, I naturally wonder about others, such as stabilizing second-level administrators and devolving authority to them; concentrating resources on bottom-up teacher development; focusing attention on smaller, strategically chosen portions of the system; or developing new structures to mobilize communities.

The challenge is literally immense. If the system were subdivided into 10 districts, there would still be 100,000 children in each. Would educational mission be clearer and have greater support in those smaller units? Of course, part of the reason decentralization wasn't more successful in the 1970s was that the quality of local governing boards was so uneven. That would still be a concern. And engaging some communities is easier said than done, as my Alaska colleague would attest.

As I reflect, furthermore, I think that a strong collective understanding of mission may have to develop as much bottom up, person by person and school by school, as top down. Recalling Seymour Sarason's (1990) observation that schools don't change because they're essentially about the power relationships among the individuals in them, I reflect that no system is better than its people, and that's where meaningful progress may have to start.

The challenges are huge, but I have to believe that school communities can develop a collective sense of mission through authentic and inventive give-and-take. What is required, are time, patience, and exceptional skill, as well as an ability to wring politics out of the system long enough to consider issues on their educational merits. That's all.

RENEWING SCHOOL MISSION

I still haven't resolved the problem I started out with: We Americans don't really agree on what we want education to do or to be. Is it even possible to reach some meaningful consensus? Are some potential missions objectively more valid than others? If so, can they prevail in a democratic system, where what's "right," however that's defined, often equates with personal interests or what is most popular?

The corporate reform movement emphasizes the economic purposes of education. Well-schooled employees make businesses competitive; competitive business creates wealth and jobs; and wealth and jobs make individual well-being possible. NCLB and Race to the Top turned that premise into a formal agenda.

Our individual and collective economic success does depend increasingly on skills and knowledge that result from a formal education. Still, tomorrow's citizens also will face other challenges. Humanity is increasingly interdependent, but we continue to devolve into tribal xenophobia. Social justice and the extremes of wealth are critical concerns. Technology may save us, but it also threatens ecosystems and life itself. And in the end, we still search for lives of fulfillment and wonder.

An education that prepares a student to solve complex global problems is sometimes the same as one that will help her become an effective worker or a contributing citizen. But that's not necessarily true.

One version of an education for the economy proposes that businesses require workers with advanced academic skills, and who are entrepreneurs, collaborators, and problem-solvers. Another version suggests that most workers need to know some math, probably up to the level of high school algebra. They have to write grammatically correct English, not ask embarrassing questions at work, and please the boss.

There are other kinds of education as well. Realizing one's own potential may have everything to do with the arts and little to do with economics. Our democracy assumes that citizens should make the common good, not just individual welfare, the standard for decisions. The humanistic ideal goes even further to imagine a state in which people dignify one another, celebrate the spirit, and ennoble the human condition.

Like the more elevated version of education for economic ends, an education for these purposes wants students to think well, to innovate, and to solve complex problems. But it also moves in different dimensions. For example, it fosters understanding of the responsibilities of citizenship. It imparts a rich sense of the human story, the natural world, and the self.

In addition, it seeks to develop what the Coalition of Essential Schools' Theodore Sizer called important "dispositions": perseverance and a desire to learn, for example. It promotes reason and values that are important in a democratic society, such as a desire to contribute. It seeks to empower, to liberate, and to inspire.

EDUCATION FOR DEMOCRACY

The education that seeks to achieve these ends is called "liberal," a term that many public schools shy away from because it can sound like a political statement. Traditionally, schools were ambivalent about whether this kind of experience was appropriate for all students. They taught skills early on, then were "comprehensive," splitting the preparation of future physicists from training for future mechanics.

For years that approach seemed only natural: Teach the basics first; children would not have to worry about material they'd never need or that might corrupt them. If ever they did get to a liberal education, therefore, it was after they were well along in the grades or even into college, when they'd been trained in skills and facts.

In the past half-century, however, new technologies have made it possible to shortcut a lot of the time-consuming trench work that occupied earlier generations: recopying papers, crunching numbers, plodding through the card catalog. In addition, we've come to understand that most people can learn big ideas when they are very young. That's what Jerome Bruner (1966), the eminent cognitive psychologist, meant when he said that any important idea can be taught to any student at some meaningful level.

For example, consider the principle that all life is interconnected and interdependent. By weaving this basic concept into increasingly complex content over a period of years, a curriculum (and good teaching) should enable children to make connections between what they already know and the new information. This process will enable them to make meaning of what they're learning. Not only that, but ideally it will motivate them to explore their personal interests (e.g., to examine the impact of development on a local wetland) and to learn more.

Traditionally, this kind of experience was reserved for students in the academic track. Those in general or vocational programs were more likely to go on studying basics (how to write the five-paragraph essay) and to receive skill training (hairdressing or food service). The challenge now is to endow all our young with capacities (and the personal rewards) associated with a liberal education, even though the subject matter may not always be traditionally academic.

LIBERAL LEARNING

Since at least the 1970s, efforts to promote liberal learning in the schools have been complicated by a debate about whether education should be a process of learning skills and content or of learning to think well. The education philosopher and University of Chicago president Robert Maynard Hutchins (1936) described the tension between these objectives when he said that every American should learn a body of knowledge, "everywhere one and the same," but that instead of filling students' heads with facts, the goal was to teach them to think (p. 166).

Content advocates and concept advocates drew up academic battle lines in the 1970s and 1980s, when universities were riven by disputes about whose history and literature (White males, women, African Americans) to teach and whose perspectives mattered. In the schools, the issues were somewhat different. Conservatives said teachers were abandoning the traditional academic core in favor of trendy fluff. Liberals said real learning was about thinking well, not absorbing masses of content.

(Much of this debate was divorced from reality. Generations of students had memorized math and science formulas and vocabulary without understanding their significance. They studied the Civil War and more lately Civil Rights without ever encountering ideas that might prompt reflection or discomfort. For thousands of children, dismal reality was Ferris Bueller's teacher droning, "Can anyone remember this legislation? Anyone . . . Anyone? The Hawley-Smoot Tariff Act . . .")

In the end, the content–concept argument was based on a false dichotomy. Both knowing and thinking are important, and each makes the other possible. You can't reason well about nothing. Content has meaning only if you can think well about it. A liberal education is a conversation; it furthers both content knowledge *and* discriminating thought.

The dispute over content and thinking consumed significant air time in the world of elementary and secondary schooling. This and other debates over less essential issues obscured a fundamental problem of mission, one that endures. Most of us don't think much at all about the purposes of education. Yet excellent schools must be clear about what they are trying to achieve, and their publics must believe in them.

Education today is rife with strategies and "solutions" that fail to address its underlying problems. A truly important challenge for communities and their leaders in the new century is to articulate and gather in support of an educational vision that is decent, generous, and profound. America's children and the nation itself deserve no less.

CHAPTER 9

THE PROBLEM OF TEACHING

After the testing focus of the Bush years, the Obama administration declared that its priority was better teaching. The change was welcome. Self-evidently, but also according to research, teaching is the most important in-school influence on learning. Other nations like poster child Finland were investing heavily in their teachers.

Not in the United States, however, where calls to contain or reduce teacher salaries and benefits were widespread, especially after the economic downturn of 2008. America offered teachers sentimental tribute. Nonetheless, the profession historically had low status and was poorly paid.

In the 19th century, a growing population had generated demand for teachers, which ordinarily would have driven wages upward. But a large source of untapped labor existed in the form of thousands of young, unmarried women who wanted to escape rural isolation and urban poverty. Teaching was a step up from the gritty, boring, and sometimes dangerous life of factory or farm work.

The large supply of candidates depressed salaries. Teaching paid less than unskilled male labor and about the same as a woman could make on the factory floor (Lebergott, 1960). (In 1866, for instance, Scarsdale's lone teacher, Eliza Allgood, received an annual salary of $156, approximately $1 a day [Hansen, 1954]. In the same year, a common laborer earned roughly $437 or about $1.56 a day in a longer work year [Lebergott, 1960].)

These economic realities ensured that the nation's teachers would be overwhelmingly female, a fact that both reflected and defined the work's status. Many of the women who taught were bright and dedicated, but for decades large numbers had only a 2-year education beyond high school. Later, only a minority majored in academic subjects (as opposed to education) in college.

With the possible exception of the Depression years, when jobs were scarce and teaching was attractive, this professional profile persisted into the mid-1900s. By the late 1960s, able, educated women were entering other professions. Although there's disagreement about the strength of today's teacher talent pool (Mourshad et al., 2010; Strauss, 2011), it's generally acknowledged that America's top college graduates don't usually become schoolteachers.

Despite these obstacles, some school districts assembled strong faculties. The process took intelligence, energy, and time. Money helped. In Scarsdale, voters elected their first female school board member in 1907. Prepared as a teacher, Elizabeth Caldwell Fountain encouraged professional development and promoted smaller classes. Her views were countercultural, and they would be for decades. In the 1930s, a letter to the editor in a local newspaper likened a good teacher to a good maid.

Scarsdale teachers brought attention to the district in the progressive 1920s. Then, in 1933, as the school board and superintendent backed away from a number of controversial innovations, the new high school principal arrived with a mandate to create the public equivalent of an elite college preparatory school. Throughout, however, the district's emphasis on quality teaching was a constant.

By the late 1940s, a number of the high school's teachers were liberal arts majors; the education they offered was rooted in liberal learning. A few years later, a local campaign to purge the schools of "red-fascist propaganda" forced the school board to re-examine its commitment to this tradition. In an unfolding drama that received national attention, the board upheld the teachers' right to choose their own texts. Voters overwhelmingly returned the incumbent trustees to office.

By affirming academic freedom in the "battle of the books," the board endorsed teachers' authority over their practice. Still later, a new superintendent, Archibald Shaw, would look back and describe the essence of a Scarsdale education as "the real necessity of children's contact with real teachers."

SCHOLAR, ARTIST, ENTREPRENEUR

In the nation's great private schools and in the liberal arts colleges that Scarsdale wanted to emulate, teachers were academics first and foremost. Their work was serious business, their purpose to transmit important knowledge and to teach students to think well. It seemed self-evident that when instructors knew and were enthusiastic about their subjects, their pupils would learn.

In this tradition, teaching was an art, and training in curriculum or teaching methods was merely vocational, not the stuff of true scholarship. Many of its practitioners would have thought it perverse to turn what they viewed as a personal, creative activity into a semi-science. And they were not entirely wrong. Teaching *was* mysterious. Nobody knew how to produce excellent teachers in any consistent way.

   Little practice could be anchored in hard research or science. Neither was it possible to transfer professional expertise consistently. Entry standards for teacher education programs were modest. Schools of education commonly admitted large percentages of applicants. Often, teacher training was a university's cash cow, generating tuition to support other, less profitable programs.

   When they were hiring teachers, superintendents and principals typically looked for certain personal qualities (high energy, enthusiasm) and past performance to predict who would be effective. The idea was to hire great people, offer them support when asked, and then let each superstar shimmer in her own arc of the instructional firmament. In reality, no constellation consists entirely of superstars. The quality of performance varied widely.

   Schools continued to draw from a shallow talent pool. In some, teachers were expected to follow highly defined curriculums and rigid instructional calendars. Administrators talked about "inservicing" staff as if they were passive receptacles and trained them in specific strategies, such as scripted teaching and the Madeline Hunter Method. New approaches passed in and out of fashion. Research about their effectiveness was often inconclusive and contradictory.

   As a practical matter, a lot of teaching was pedestrian and conformist. Still, the tradition of the brilliant independent scholar/artist endured in places like Scarsdale and in districts quite unlike it. Enlightened administrators encouraged teachers to capitalize on their individual strengths and interests. One 5th-grade teacher might cover American Indians, while others did the Revolutionary War or local history in the 1700s.

   A Scarsdale High School teacher who was new to the school in 1964 remembers what happened that year: "The department chair introduced me around and showed me the book room. She didn't give me a curriculum; I thought she didn't want to overwhelm me. After a few weeks, she still hadn't told me what to do, and I was starting to worry. So I asked when she was going to give me the syllabus. She looked at me—she seemed surprised—and said, 'But that's why we hired *you*, my dear.'"

   This system—or the lack thereof—seemed to work in many schools, or to work well enough, at least. As we saw in Chapter 7, children in some communities benefited from the self-reinforcing cycle of education, motivation, and resourcing. In any number of districts, structural innovations that included smaller schools, "houses" within larger buildings, and adviser systems enabled teachers to know students well and to collaborate with one another. Personal connections, more than any written curriculum or code, reinforced expectations and helped to coordinate instruction.

PROFESSIONAL

In the 1950s and 1960s, the quality of instruction in Scarsdale reflected not only individual teachers' strengths and organizational structures but also a maturing school culture. Teachers, administrators, and board members saw one another not so much as managers or workers but as people. Faculty had meaningful authority over their practice, and most responded by holding themselves to high standards.

Building on this foundation, and with board support, teachers sought to transform their work into a true profession, one with a transferable craft, autonomy, and self-regulation.

Two developments were influential. In the 1960s, researchers were uncovering new knowledge about ways to improve schools and teaching. This work informed efforts to build a culture in which teachers were constantly learning and growing. Also, faculty leaders identified with an idealistic strain of the emerging labor movement in which unions were a path to professional status and to quality instruction.

New York State's Taylor Law formalized public labor relations in 1967. Scarsdale superintendent Donald Emery called for a union–management collaboration that would be "professional in nature and avoid the pitfalls of traditional . . . negotiations" (Rothschild, 1977). This new relationship would not be stress-free, but the parties cooperated. The community was interested in good teaching and good outcomes, not labor strife. Funding was sufficient to smooth many of the frictions that often sidetracked teaching and learning elsewhere.

Consistent with Emery's injunction, teachers and administrators explored the possibilities of professional collaboration. In the last third of the 20th century, teachers served on search committees and mentored the newly hired. They took responsibility for their own growth; in 1968, Scarsdale created a self-governing Teachers Institute for continuing professional education. Also typifying leading-edge thinking of the time were new methods of performance evaluation and a "career lattice" (or career ladder) plan that allowed teachers to take on leadership roles outside the classroom.

The Teachers Institute grew from a vision of teachers as professionals who voluntarily undertake self-development throughout their careers. A policy board shaped a program of graduate-level courses, lectures, and workshops on topics ranging from international education to critical and creative thinking. In a given year, between 80% and 90% of teachers took part.

The "career lattice" enabled teachers to take on new responsibilities without having to move into administration. They led departments, programs, and committees; they were teachers of teachers, new-teacher mentors, curriculum specialists, and staff developers. There was no Mandarin caste of administrators; a relatively "flat" organization was generally responsive to grassroots issues and needs.

Also, instead of going through a checklist evaluation, tenured teachers could focus 2 out of 3 years on self-development projects. Typically, these projects involved inquiry in an area of interest or need: how questioning techniques affected student motivation, for example. Freed from having to evaluate large numbers of people annually, principals concentrated on a smaller number of the nontenured and on any tenured faculty who were in real difficulty.

By the 1990s, approaches like these had created what was called "a learning community," in which new ideas and ongoing professional opportunities helped teachers stay intellectually alive and productive throughout their careers.

Still, the model of teacher-as-professional was imperfect, just as the paradigm of scholarly/artistic teaching had been. While classroom instruction was strong overall, its quality still varied. For good and for ill, students in different classes had different experiences. There could be disconnects between what they learned one year and the next. And while the faculty collectively embraced a highly professional ethic, they had few ways to hold individual outliers accountable.

THE PROFESSION TODAY

The quality of the nation's teaching force varied even more. There still was no definitive core of knowledge or skills that every teacher should acquire: no hard science, no authoritative National Academy of Education. To the contrary, schools of education, individual professors, and independent consultants were in competition and had little incentive to agree on anything.

Students in different teacher preparation programs studied different material. Standards varied. Professors with doctorates taught some education courses; teachers from nearby school districts taught others. Some students received clinical training—extended classroom coaching by an expert mentor, for instance. Others didn't. The duration and quality of teaching internships varied.

Discussion about an educational parallel to medical board certification became reality in 1987, when a National Board for Professional Teaching Standards was created. Teachers earned certification by submitting videotapes, portfolios of their work and their students' efforts, and other evidence of their own performance. In theory, the result would be an elite group of highly qualified practitioners and a narrow supply of top-tier job applicants.

In practice, however, an aspiring teacher could still take one of many different routes to employment. Most districts made little distinction between board-certified teachers and others; they continued to hire from the general pool, often with an eye to minimizing cost. Board certification was also time-consuming and expensive. In the end, professional pride was the main incentive to pursue it.

Once teachers entered the classroom, few districts invested substantially in their development. Few places adopted the Asian practice of using time from the work day for professional discussion, for instance. Often, novices were isolated in their rooms, coping with 25 students or more. Support took the form of an occasional visit from a department chair whose own schedule left little time to cultivate the newcomer's skills. Inservice education was likely to be a single-event lecture or a workshop that involved no actual practice.

Furthermore, professional development was usually one of the first areas to be cut from budgets when the economy weakened. The public often seemed to assume that teachers should be fully trained when they started. After that, they were to stand and deliver. Under the circumstances, it was hard to understand how teaching could improve on a broad national scale.

In the early 2000s, the George W. Bush administration decided that the answer was to regulate a first-rate teaching force into existence. NCLB accordingly proclaimed that all teachers must be "highly qualified." Since real improvement would have required money, imagination, effort, and time, a number of states adopted the equally simple expedient of declaring that their teachers were highly qualified.

Seven years later, the Obama administration had an opportunity to take a more productive approach. Following the 2008 election, however, hardline advisers to the White House promoted the familiar corporate prescription of accountability, metrics, charter schools, and confrontation with unions. "Soft" reformers emphasized the need to build teachers' knowledge and skills.

When Race to the Top went into effect in July 2009, the harder edge was far more apparent. Influential corporations, newspaper editorials, and politicians had promoted get-tough measures like teacher rating and merit-pay schemes. As always, these prescriptions were easy to understand and superficially appealing, relatively easy to translate into regulation and to monitor.

The strategy worked on a deficit model that implicitly reflected a mistrust of educators. As I have said, it assumed that poor teaching was often the function of a slacking, civil-service mentality. Notionally, principals' and department heads' failure to hold their subordinates accountable was a major part of the problem. That was why most teachers ended up with "satisfactory" ratings, according to the theory.

The federal solution was to mandate a mechanical evaluation process that would force supervisors to be more rigorous. Race to the Top required states to "differentiate [teachers' and principals'] effectiveness using multiple rating categories that take into account student growth" (USED, 2009). In New York State, that was 40 points for student scores on standardized tests, 31 points for classroom observations, and 29 "other" points, each category further divided into subcategories with point designations.

Theoretically, this "objective" system was superior to evaluation plans that placed greater emphasis on human judgment, which was imperfect or irresolute. Teaching could become more like assembly-line work, a process of performing specified functions within quantified parameters. The metrics also could be structured to render a certain percentage of workers ineffective and to reward others.

In practice, the approach had serious shortcomings. As I said in Chapter 5, it produced precise performance ratings that were invalid or absurd. Further, the attempt to substitute a mechanical, formulaic evaluation system for human judgment created its own problems. For example, a teacher could amass enough points in several different performance categories to be "satisfactory," even if a single, truly serious deficiency outweighed her strengths. (Recall the social studies teacher who demeaned her students.)

To be fair, substandard teaching sometimes did reflect evaluators' aversion to hard decisions, but many other forces were also at work. As we've seen, serious performance problems often defied easy identification, description, or documentation, or effective coaching. They took time to understand and address. Frequently, supervisors had to try to manage the most difficult cases while also evaluating 15, 20, or more other people, teaching, and/or running a department or a school.

Too often, supervisors also lacked good training, so that they did not truly understand the performance standards they were supposed to use or lacked the skills needed to address problems. In addition, relatively few school districts funded progressive human resources programs: mentoring or counseling services that supported a struggling teacher before supervisors shifted to more formal and confrontational discipline.

More and better staff development, more and better training for supervisors, and improved support systems certainly would have helped improve teaching. But instead of promoting or funding these kinds of efforts, the USED left the "soft" work of reform to the states, which generally passed it on to the schools.

The strategy reflected federal priorities, respected the states' authority, and avoided the significant financial commitment that a broad, intensive investment in teacher education or quality supervision would have required. It also acknowledged tacitly the impossibility of exercising tight, centralized control over hundreds of thousands of individuals in thousands of different places.

But, in addition, the approach failed to adequately address two critical issues: the global learning gap and the variation in teaching quality that existed everywhere.

The global learning gap was the divide between the education children received and the one they would need to succeed in an interdependent world. Even the nation's high-performing schools, if they were honest, had to admit that they didn't systematically cultivate deep understanding of other cultures or global issues, and that they did not do enough to develop qualities like independence or curiosity.

The uneven quality of teaching, as Harvard professor Richard Elmore (2008) had pointed out, was an issue in every school in America. Students in one classroom could be engaged in higher-level critical thinking while those next door memorized facts. In the past, a less than successful response had been to try to standardize curriculum or teaching methods. But was there some better way to minimize unhelpful variation *and also* promote the individuality that made teaching great?

THE GLOBAL LEARNING GAP AND VARIABLE TEACHING QUALITY

What did teachers need to know and do to offer students a global education? Especially when access to limitless information was instant, factual knowledge was less significant for its own sake and more significant for supporting or informing a larger point. So teachers had to be especially expert in their fields to help students sort big ideas and extract meaningful information from all the background noise.

They also had to be adept at helping students develop skills like creative thinking, problem-finding and -solving, inquiry, and innovation. Conventional wisdom held that these properties developed as a natural consequence of academic study: by learning math, people came to think logically. But curriculum alone didn't teach people to think well. That required good teachers.

Children were stubbornly, inconveniently, and brilliantly individual. Their abilities and interests differed. They weren't all ready to learn the same thing at the same time, and they didn't all learn the same way. They could be motivated by emotion as much as by reason. Often, social interactions were more important to them than academic pursuits. They might or might not share the school's or teacher's goals.

Schools organized these individuals into classes whose dynamics resembled an atomic chain reaction: ideas and actions ricocheting unpredictably and changing one another. As a Scarsdale teacher said, "We [teachers] have to use everything the environment has to offer. Maybe I use a word a child didn't know and he figures it out and has a new word, or I see the expression of someone struggling and understand more about how people handle frustration. There are endless iterations of this type of learning."

A novice teacher coped with these fluid conditions using a curriculum, a daily lesson plan, and whatever classroom strategies she'd learned in school. The expert, to paraphrase Horace Mann (1840/1989), perceived how far a student understood, and what, in the natural order, was the next step she must take. He could discover and solve her exact difficulty at the time. He was also sensitive to the flow of interactions and of interplay within the group. He responded in the moment to multiple, emerging understandings, feelings, and actions. No fixed progression of actions produced good results.

Nonetheless, accomplished teachers did have a craft that could be transmitted from one person to another. There were hundreds of teaching strategies, a wide array of classroom management skills, content-specific pedagogy in each academic discipline at every grade level, and skills that were involved in collaborating with colleagues—on analysis of student data and student work, for example (Saphier, Speca, & Gower, 2008).

Traditionally, teachers learned some of this craft through informal conversations among colleagues—when they could find time. They also acquired it from courses, lectures, and workshops, a bit like learning to play basketball by listening to a speech. Unsurprisingly, these efficient and relatively cheap methods of instruction left trainees with fragmentary recollections of what they had heard, ideas they would understand only partially and implement imperfectly.

Forward-thinking educators sought better approaches.

Formal "action research" protocols enabled teachers to critique their own work and to assess the impact of new curriculums or methods. "Critical friends" was a collaborative group process of evaluating classrooms and sharing feedback about the observations. Lesson study engaged groups of five to seven in collaborative lesson planning; one would teach the class while the rest observed and later analyzed the work.

As I said earlier, more progressive school districts also began to take more thorough approaches to performance evaluation. For example, a team approach to supervision involved several classroom observers, who visited a teacher separately or together during the year. The team met periodically to review evidence from the observations, teaching plans, materials, and students' work. A lead supervisor coordinated their feedback and coached the teacher.

Activities like these were analogous to the clinical training that occurs in hospitals—and in batting cages. Teachers had to reflect systematically on their classroom moves, and they received timely, detailed feedback. The approach was people- and time-intensive, and costly. A Scarsdale could shift and add resources—so that three staff development coaches supported implementation of a new elementary school math program, for instance. But that kind of effort was unusual.

In addition to strengthening practitioners' academic backgrounds and teaching skills, a third strategy for improving instruction was to improve assessment. Knowing what a student did and did not understand, a teacher obviously would be in a better position to "solve his exact difficulty at the time." But as we've seen, when assessment was about raising scores, there was little incentive to teach or evaluate what couldn't be tested well: important global competencies that cut across grades or the traditional disciplinary "silos," for instance.

Still, the focus on mandated testing didn't completely derail efforts to build better assessments or to use them to improve instruction. For instance, a 5th-grade "capstone" project in Scarsdale evaluated children's ability to identify a significant question and carry out a study involving higher-order thinking skills and technology. After discussing the film *Flags of Our Fathers* with his mother, for instance, one boy decided to research the Battle of Iwo Jima. The study led him online to a World War II veteran in New Orleans.

The Marine, then in his eighties, sent the student pictures of his landing craft and black sand from the beach where his unit had landed. A video interview of the boy is deeply moving, not only because of the topic's inherent power, but because of the poignant connection between distant places and different generations, symbolized by the sand the student shows his interviewer near the end.

What did the boy learn? He got involved in a field he found meaningful. He formulated a significant question: "What was the Battle of Iwo Jima and why was it important?" He used technology to gather information from many sources, scoured it, integrated it, and prepared an organized, analytical response to his question. His response took written, verbal, and visual forms. These products gave evidence of how well he'd mastered several important global competencies.

A teacher could have used this information to extend the boy's learning, to help him improve the questions he asked his primary source in New Orleans, for instance. More broadly, the results of student research also helped teachers collectively. In early iterations of the capstone project, for example, some children picked topics such as "the polar bear," while others identified essential questions. Recognizing the difference, teachers began to concentrate on helping their students ask good questions.

The capstone project was a relatively traditional way of evaluating and of improving teaching and curriculum. It was nontraditional because it began with student interest, as opposed to a teacher assignment; because teachers consciously concentrated on critical thinking and creativity; and because they collectively focused on helping students develop and use evidence to make a case. The final product wasn't final; it was also a platform to build pupils' thinking further.

Still, despite such efforts, the quality of instruction continued to vary from classroom to classroom, school to school, all across the nation, leading back to the question I posed earlier: How can we improve consistency and coordination, and simultaneously nurture the individuality that makes teaching great?

One starting point is to think of the problem as an opportunity to forge a consensus on essentials that should be consistent and areas that should be subject to individual judgment. For example, what five big ideas and skills will we all emphasize? How will we know whether our students' critical thinking is growing stronger?

Discussions like that require extensive give-and-take. Differing views and personalities are hard to reconcile. The daily work of running schools and classrooms is full-time. The larger the school or district, the greater the challenge.

In Scarsdale, after a year of discussion, teachers and administrators agreed to concentrate on thinking skills and complex, interdisciplinary problem solving. They began to work toward agreement on the meaning of terms: When we talk about critical thinking, do we mean the same thing?

Other questions followed: "Where and how are we fostering good thinking, how good is it, and how do we know?" "What can students in the world's strongest schools do?" "How well can our students perform, relative to that standard?" The last two of these topics were especially mysterious, since international tests produced scores, but little information about the work students overseas actually did in class.

A number of teachers agreed to examine student work together. That presumably would help them develop a common appreciation for what a term like *creative thinking* actually meant and looked like in practice. From there, they would work toward consensus about where to be more consistent and how to improve their work.

However, there were no good external benchmarks—samples of high-quality student work from schools in the United States and overseas—to anchor judgments about local students' work. As a result, members of the district administrative team began to think about how to form an international network of public and independent schools that could help develop this kind of information, an effort I will discuss further in Chapter 11.

Looking back at these and all the other efforts of a century in Scarsdale, one had to be both impressed and daunted by the time, human energy, and money that had been invested in effective teaching. And after all that effort, the work was still very much in progress. How many other districts or schools had made—or been able to make—a similar commitment? How would quality of teaching in the United States improve markedly if they did not?

CHAPTER 10

A LEARNING COMMUNITY

How do school faculties become more than collections of individuals; how do they become teams of people who strive to achieve common goals? What causes them to want to stretch themselves and to improve?

THE STATE OF THE SCHOOLS: 2000

When I became Scarsdale's superintendent in 1998, student performance really was "demonstrably excellent," as the high school math chair told me. Everyone graduated; 95% of each senior class went to 4-year colleges; over 55% were being admitted to colleges rated "most competitive." Teaching was thoughtful and often engaging.

After I'd had time to get the lay of this new land, I wrote a think piece to provoke conversation about the future. In my view, the main challenge was to capitalize on the strengths of the district's independent, able teachers, so the institution as a collective entity would grow. When I circulated my paper to a small group of people, though, it didn't get the response I'd hoped for. Allowing that my intentions might be good, the union president told me I was on the brink of violating an important norm.

My ideas would intimidate teachers, she said. They were tantamount to a mandate. In Scarsdale, new concepts bubbled up from the bottom. Outsiders' experience really didn't apply. In fact, the superintendent's main job was to appreciate and celebrate the excellent work everyone was already doing. My paper would devalue them and generate anger and mistrust. Backlash was sure to follow.

A letter from the faculty organization executive committee followed. Carefully, it expressed dismay at my insensitivity and politely explained reality: I'd failed to respect "the Scarsdale Way." I knew I shouldn't take the rebuff personally, but still . . . . I was only trying to start a discussion. I realized that, of course, the union president was showing me she was a force to be reckoned with. At the same time, she might not just be posturing, and the executive committee sounded sincere.

116

They weren't being unreasonable. Why argue with what worked? And why not just encourage people to go on doing what they obviously did well? As in many high-performing schools, objective problems were few; nobody had to deal with the stresses created by extreme poverty or with challenges like high dropout rates. If some teachers were a bit defensive, the faculty were rightly proud of what they had accomplished.

The culture of the place tended to be individualistic and somewhat entrepreneurial, but while teachers regularly brought fresh ideas and approaches into their classes, the faculty as a whole were cautious about broader institutional change in departments, schools, or the district. In the view of any one individual, more comprehensive change could threaten what he or she had already built. Individuals also felt a sense of ownership for the schools: If significant change were to occur, each wanted it to reflect her or his own vision. Because this kind of culture worked, according to all the usual measures, schools like Scarsdale tended to de-emphasize command and control. Directives from the top were relatively infrequent. Significant decisions usually reflected a search for consensus.

As a result, almost any meaningful large-scale change could slow to a crawl or stop entirely. Discussion, negotiation, and compromise took time. And in Scarsdale, there wasn't a lot of it left after teachers had taught students, seen them outside of class, completed committee obligations, and finished their Teachers Institute courses. (In many districts with a trade-union culture, change also came hard; faculty organizations would actively discourage professional dialogue unless it was compensated.)

So what was the new superintendent's best course? The theory underlying much of corporate reform is that resistance to innovation is so stubborn and reflexive that change has to occur on demand. Unfortunately, the unintended consequences of this approach can be worse than the original problem. According to a different theory, effective change is most likely to occur when those who have to implement it understand and support it. That approach takes time, and some people never get on board.

In practice, the two strategies are ends of a continuum. Neither is objectively "best." Some organizations are authoritarian for understandable reasons. The military is built to respond to crisis. If a school is unstable, almost any structure may be better than none. Regardless of whether it's progressive or regressive, directive leadership may seem to be the only thing that's holding chaos at bay.

The point is that the "right" strategy depends on the context, which includes not only leaders' goals but history ("We've had five school principals in 5 years") and culture (What are the local customs, beliefs, values, traditions?). Where education is concerned, furthermore, human interactions are essential to achieving the organization's goals. And especially in organizations that are about human relations, top-down leadership is problematic.

Lasting and constructive innovation in these places typically begins with a common felt need. It depends on trust and is more likely to succeed if the people who have to make it work have concrete experience with, or can see examples of, what it might look like in practice. When innovation aligns with core institutional values, finally, the synergy can supercharge it with special energy.

So in Scarsdale, one option was to push back against what many of today's school reformers would have interpreted as self-interested resistance. I could have forced the issue: The superintendent is in charge. Send out the position paper, and if the union objects, embrace the conflict. But I had to think carefully about the objective, which was to promote self-reflection and growth. That meant we had to trust one another and be willing to take risks.

Even if I'd thought confrontation made sense, furthermore, laws and state regulations insulated teachers from top-down direction. These strictures hadn't materialized out of nowhere. Tenure was originally a way to protect schools against arbitrary management, politics, and favoritism. Similarly, unions wouldn't have existed if salaries and working conditions had been better and school boards and administrators hadn't abused their authority. Still, many of these protections had become rigid constraints in their own right.

That was the problem that frustrated former New York City chancellor Joel Klein and former Washington, DC, chancellor Michelle Rhee in the early 2000s as they tried to improve their large urban districts. Corporate reformers cheered their hardline efforts to alter work rules, end tenure, impose merit pay, and eliminate seniority. But conflict over these issues easily turned into an existential struggle between labor and management.

If you were a school superintendent anywhere in the United States, you probably empathized with Rhee's frustrations from time to time. But once she and the union became locked in a struggle for brute power, "improving teaching and learning" became a partisan battle cry. When every issue is a gut issue and conflict is unending, a leader loses effectiveness. In fact, the only entity able to work rapid change in these situations without tearing a district apart may be an outside agency like a state.

Scarsdale's experience was very different from the one in DC. Because of a long history of respectful relations, union and management were much more likely to collaborate than to conflict. The contract was thin. Work conditions like the length of the day and class size remained under board control. Teachers worked hard. And my friend the union president had a valid point: Rapid, top-down moves could have been unproductive.

While confrontation might have prompted useful discussion, it also could have led to time-wasting and divisive arguments over power, especially if union leadership were unsupportive. ("Why are you forcing this goal on us instead of that one?" "This is just another mandate that'll make it harder for me to do my job!") In addition, of course (and although it is barely conceivable), teachers might even have had more wisdom than a superintendent. So trying to be philosophical and at the same time to find some humor in the situation, I decided to trust the system.

The understood "safe" vehicle for addressing new or controversial ventures in Scarsdale was to appoint a joint administration–faculty committee. I agreed, and asked a respected neutral party to moderate discussions. What was important wasn't who stood in front of the room, but to advance the work and start a conversation. At least that's what I told myself, wondering if I was being naive.

Such was my introduction to three essential challenges of leadership.

- How could I offer a vision of the future that resonated with the district's core values? How could I engage people in the school community with that vision, so they'd stretch themselves in pursuit of it?
- How could I understand a highly complex indigenous culture and also use what I knew about education to help it progress? How could I earn trust so I could make a contribution?
- How could I keep enough critical distance to see institutional needs clearly? And how could I make the most of the institution's strengths and its wisdom in the process?

Past boards of education had set instructional objectives: to bring technology more fully into the classroom, for instance. Sometimes they'd adopted goals that were more operational: to review rising enrollments and consider their implication for building expansion, for example. In general, these prior efforts had been loosely connected to what the large majority of teachers actually did, day to day.

The union president had no problem with this arrangement. Her view evidently was that in the best of all possible worlds, superintendents and boards would benignly neglect what she called teachers' "real work": educating children. The approach recalled the wry prayer of Sholem Aleichem's Tevye: "God bless the czar and keep him . . . far away from us."

For its part, the board wanted to disencumber itself from a management role it had been drawn into playing as two permanent and two interim superintendents left, arrived, left, arrived, and left again between 1993 and 1998, when I was appointed. Some of the trustees were experienced senior business executives. Others had served on private boards. They wanted the superintendent to run the schools.

To reestablish their policy focus, we started with the mission, then identified longer-term strategic ends, setting seven objectives to start. The idea was that these somewhat generic statements (e.g., "Differentiate instruction to respond more fully to individual needs") would be broken down into more specific, more measurable objectives later on. The approach would have been unremarkable in many school districts; in Scarsdale, it was almost entirely countercultural.

In the decentralized, traditionally organized district of the early 2000s, most meaningful educational decisions occurred through a handful of counterbalancing structures, each with its own span of authority. At the high school, for instance, academic departments determined course offerings, subject content, and student groupings. To an unusual extent, each elementary school developed its own program, and coordination among them was limited.

Few if any structures addressed districtwide priorities or issues outside the bounds of the academic disciplines. For example, there were few ways for everyone to think collectively about what a goal like "love of learning" might mean or how it might be achieved. Neither did there seem to be much experience with decisions that used the welfare of the whole institution as a benchmark. A high school schedule revision proposal died, for instance, largely because each department saw the allocation of time through the lens of its own needs and interests.

"NOTHING EVER CHANGES"

In a system with few overarching structures, one that relied heavily on voluntarism and consensus, individuals could innovate with relative ease. But the farther one got from each classroom, the more the status quo seemed to prevail. Many teachers seemed to find this arrangement amiable; it also could be frustrating. As one veteran noted with asperity, "I've been here for 25 years and we keep having the same discussions and nothing ever changes."

The first joint committee meetings led to the idea of an annual progress review, a recurring opportunity for its members to think together about district initiatives. Culminating in a report to the board each June, this planning process became an established, accepted part of the calendar. While it reduced concern about the effort's turning into a series of top-down mandates, however, the cycle was mechanical, and it remained disconnected from most teachers' daily work.

In the spring of 2004, consequently, planning committee members identified four questions: "How do we identify unusual ideas and get them heard?" "How can we maintain excitement in our work?" "How can we encourage dialogue across the usual boundaries?" "How can we engage the faculty more fully?"

The district's two assistant superintendents proposed a simplified planning process: Identify a handful of clearly worded goals that would fit on one piece of paper, then involve more teachers in discussions about them, so everyone literally would "get on the same page." The new union president—her predecessor had retired—agreed that all district teachers and administrators would be invited to an expanded spring strategic-planning meeting aimed at connecting plan and practice more directly.

It was tempting to see the progress as evidence of the superintendent's profound wisdom, but more likely causes were the district's history of union–management cooperation and a union president who had taken a collaborative approach to the work. (Her predecessor, to establish her authority, I assumed, had come to a meeting early in my tenure and made a point of wanting to sit in "a big chair" instead of one of the smaller ones at the table. I offered her mine; she accepted. I later sent it to her office as a gift, tied in a large bow. I never asked her whether she appreciated the humor.)

The council of district administrators and principals endorsed the new approach, and a subcommittee proposed three objectives for the new process:

- Recast district goals in plain language to reflect the faculty's real work.
- Make the new process more organic and authentic.
- Ensure that work on the goals reflected the best thinking in Scarsdale and beyond.

"ON THE SAME PAGE"

Attracting about a third of the faculty, an inaugural district planning meeting approved a reworked and shortened version of the district goals in 2005. These were:

- To inspire a love of learning
- To prepare graduates for success and leadership in the interdependent world
- To promote an ethic of social contribution

The goals were interconnected, and each could be said to flow from the others. A love of learning would very probably help people succeed in an interdependent world, for example.

The goals and the student experience meshed—episodically. Traditional curriculums in subjects like math and English were relatively coordinated, especially in the departmentalized secondary schools. However, neither administrators nor teachers could have said with real certainty how well the district was preparing students for the global community or whether teachers were using any approaches consistently to instill a love of learning.

Nonetheless, the efforts to simplify the goals and involve more people directly in the process were important. In 2008, most teachers and administrators could have told a visitor what at least two of the three district goals were. The shift was significant because of what it wasn't: a result of memorization or public relations. Because the professional staff had gotten into the messy business of working with the ideas, the ideas had begun to be concrete, to take on meaning in people's minds.

At the Spring 2008 strategic-planning meeting, 70-some teachers and administrators examined literature on 21st-century learning and agreed on the value of teaching a core of academic topics that they specified, as well as "higher-order" skills (analysis, synthesis, problem solving), technology fluency, and dispositions such as perseverance. In fact, they had tried to impart many of these things for years. That was what a strong liberal education was about.

Less clear was how, when, or the degree to which students developed these abilities. Teachers knew what went on in their own classes, but there was relatively little understanding of what others did. The so-called "higher-order" thinking capacities were implicit in many or all of the disciplines, but there was no consistent way of evaluating how well students had mastered many of them. Everyone and no one was ultimately responsible for teaching them.

The search for coherence also led to discussions about the district's leadership structure. Administrators, the union president, and the head of the Teachers Institute, working with a Columbia University professor, discussed distributed leadership: a process of drawing on their individual talents to advance the strategic plan, regardless of their job titles. They also wrestled with the tension between fostering teachers' individuality and giving every student access to a common core of knowledge and practice.

CHINA, THE ECONOMY, A WORK PLAN

While the conversations continued in the following months, several other important developments occurred. In July 2008, I visited schools in China. That fall, a new assistant superintendent suggested that we develop a more structured work plan. Later in the autumn, the U.S. economy began to come apart.

In China, one of my hosts shared the following story: In the early 2000s, the government decided that Harbin—a city of several millions that many Americans have never heard of—should expand.

As a result, there now were hundreds of acres of new apartments, schools, and businesses across the river. A new university rose from nothing in just 2 years. The classroom buildings, dorms, museum, and laboratories were enormous.

"How did they get it done?" I asked, thinking public bidding, OSHA, labor unions. "Let me tell you," said the man. "A year ago, Harbin was applying to host the World University Games. A man on the selection panel said, 'How can you be ready? You don't have half the facilities you need.' Our leader replied, 'You have the full assurance of the Chinese Government that it will be done.' The man started to interject, when another panel member interrupted. 'I don't think you understand,' he said. 'If the Chinese Government says it'll be ready, it *will* be ready.'"

Immense ambition, resources, and energy. Common cause. National pride and a spirit of sacrifice for the greater good. All things were possible. The only way to appreciate the purposefulness was to experience it—or maybe to have been in the United States during and shortly after World War II. If you can recall the few days after 9/11, but without the fear, you can begin to capture the feeling. How could a fragmented and self-absorbed America compete?

Historically, the United States has been distinguished by its innovation and creativity, its ability to find new solutions to problems with no clear answers. We look at our public schools and see disarray. Other nations look at us and want to find out how we develop original thinkers and problem-solvers. So that's what I said to Scarsdale's faculty in September 2008.

The available measures—state tests, SATs, even AP tests—said our students were as well educated as the strongest pupils in America's strongest public schools. But the available measures also told us relatively little about how well they had mastered the higher-level capacities that are so important in the emerging world. And the results did not tell us how well our students were educated relative to the best in the world.

Scarsdale sophomores recently had taken the PISA test of their critical-thinking and problem-solving skills. The good news was that if Scarsdale had been a country, it would have been the highest scoring on the globe. More ambiguously, the average score was at the fourth level on a test with six levels. In level six were problems lacking clear right answers and asking students to figure out what the problem was.

So I told the faculty that America was resilient. And the challenge from the East could be overstated. Nonetheless, I felt a sense of urgency as I took part in discussions of our students' thinking and problem-solving abilities. It seemed clear that more faculty conversation in the abstract wasn't likely to move the effort forward. I wrote several drafts of a memo in which I tried to consolidate the gist of discussions for the administrative team's review.

Considering the reaction to my position paper some years before, I thought it was hopeful when the group encouraged me to develop the draft for faculty reaction. Possibly, the evolution was a sign that I'd earned a measure of trust; equally, I might just have come to seem harmless, the Scarsdale Way having worn me down over the years. Of course, both things could have been true. I began rewriting.

The draft was ready by November 2008. For me, meanwhile, the emerging economic crisis was summoning up depressing echoes of earlier hard times I'd been through. Frustrated taxpayers would target the school budget. Finances would undergo minute scrutiny. We would hear impassioned public rhetoric about financial peril and the need for austerity. The press and the politicians would pile on. No matter what economies we created, there would be calls for more cuts.

At the same time, quality education was ever more vital to students' futures. Good schools also gave value to property. With economics fueling a sense of crisis, residents especially would need to understand the consequences of budget and program decisions. Suddenly, the district's strategic vision was important in ways that couldn't have been anticipated just a few months before.

AN EDUCATION FOR TOMORROW

The final document, "A Scarsdale Education for the Future," described "a new core curriculum" in areas teachers had endorsed during the previous spring's strategic-planning exercise: academic content, thinking skills, technological knowledge, and "dispositions" including empathy and respect. It said that graduates would need to rely on the best of traditional scholarship and teaching.

"A Scarsdale Education" also described the importance of studies that could cut across or fall outside the traditional disciplines. This part of the new core curriculum involved critical thinking and solving "nonstandard" problems like the economic meltdown. It would promote an ethic of service. The paper identified where this core was already being taught: AT and the capstone project, for instance.

After a review by groups of administrators, other curriculum leaders, departments, and faculties, a revised document went to the May 2009 strategic-planning meeting. Participants concurred that the schools did a good job of imparting academic content but developed students' thinking skills less purposefully. The upshot was a plan to use conference days and faculty and department meetings to develop more common understandings of what terms like *critical thinking* meant.

ORGANIZATIONAL CULTURE AND CHANGE

Strategic planning in Scarsdale had evolved, but the evolution had been consistent with the Scarsdale Way. District leaders—administrators and teachers—had framed issues, while deliberations became increasingly inclusive. They'd built on the strengths of existing programs and on teacher interest. Almost mysteriously, furthermore, events like my trip to China and unplanned contacts with outside experts had added energy to the effort at propitious moments.

In September 2009, 60-some Scarsdale administrators and other program leaders considered the plan and the challenges posed by the recession. They also discussed the fact that 2009 was the 225th year a public school had existed in Scarsdale. A celebration of "Scarsdale 225" and the ideas in the strategic plan symbolized, respectively, the district's traditional quality and the reasons for enhancing it in the future.

In November, teachers saw videos highlighting their colleagues' efforts to develop thinking skills: a history fair that was also the final learning assessment in grade 9, for instance. Then, in smaller groups, they assessed the videos' relevance to their own work. In the months that followed, administrators, whole faculties, and academic departments examined and selected evidence to show the accreditors who were due to arrive in May for one of their regular reviews of the district's efforts.

All this effort could have been mandated, and some of it might have welled up from the classroom. But neither approach would have generated the interest a more evolutionary process had created. Formal and informal leaders throughout the organization had worked together to encourage comprehensive involvement and to promote systemic change.

Those with a system-wide perspective—administrators, union officers, and some teachers—had asked broad questions and provided
"provocations": critical-thinking exercises or ideas for discussion. These
frameworks offered a structure for faculty discussion, without requiring
dumb compliance. They were open enough to invite independent thinking and creativity.

The Scarsdale culture of idiosyncrasy, entrepreneurship, voluntarism,
consensus-seeking, and continuous learning had absorbed change, and it
had been changed by the rigor of the planning processes. While it was resilient, it was also delicate. If leadership had been more directive, teachers
more independent and entrepreneurial, consensus-building less effective,
for instance, progress could have stalled.

Going forward, the challenge was to balance individuality and
synergy. Longstanding structures like academic departments and conference days helped to increase communication. Newer ones like the
strategic-planning meeting led to other useful innovations. One elementary school principal had taken the lead in encouraging teachers
to visit one another's classrooms, for example. Now it invited faculty
from other buildings. "We are hoping this will jump-start the process
of breaking down the barriers between levels and schools and at the
same time develop an understanding of what goes on at the elementary
level," said the principal.

The district also made use of its think tanks to generate ideas and energy. To improve work on global issues, for instance, the Interdependence
Institute—an interest group of administrators and teachers—brought
overseas educators into the schools and sent Scarsdale teachers and students abroad. Meanwhile, outside institutions like the Lincoln Center Institute provided perspectives that helped to validate and challenge local
thinking.

Another source of new ideas was a partnership with Columbia University. At one meeting, a professor mused that the strategic plan might
be more complete if it included a Scarsdale theory of how students learn.
The discussion also helped to clarify distinctions between creative thinking (a process that could, perhaps, be broken into parts and taught) and
creativity (an intuitive act that may not be teachable but that is more
likely to flourish in a favorable environment).

Serendipitously, also, Scarsdale had adopted a new elementary school
math program developed in Singapore. The initiative led to a contact
with Ban Har Yeap, a Singaporean expert in teaching critical thinking and
problem solving. The connection led principals and teachers to become
involved in lesson study, the collaborative process of planning classes,
observing them, and coaching the participants.

AN EDUCATION FOR TOMORROW, TODAY

What had the strategic plan achieved? Evidence of meaningful organizational change: a redesigned capstone project and 8th-grade, year-end assessments; a new global citizenship class; substantial teacher involvement in lesson study; a makeover of curriculum to include more problem solving. Underlying these specific developments was a renewed sense of energy and momentum. Professional staff had seen the need for more common focus. Intentional, explicit cross-grade and cross-school interactions were more common.

When the accreditation team arrived in May, it offered a number of observations. First, while there is no shortage of talk about "21st-century skills," people may not agree on what terms like *creative thinking* mean. There is even less consensus about how to develop such capacities—or whether some of them can be taught at all. Nor is there accord on what might constitute satisfactory evidence that students have acquired them.

Second, Scarsdale teachers had courageously confronted the challenge of trying to answer these questions. The process of building new knowledge couldn't be reduced to a structured plan with a predefined conclusion. Like most pure research, leading-edge exploration had to be a matter of taking one step, then seeing where the next one seemed to lead.

Third, a critical mass of people were "on the same page" about priorities. Others were coming on board. More important to me was the observation that instead of being self-satisfied, teachers were quietly proud of the progress they'd made and serious about continuing. Their achievements almost certainly were embedded more deeply than if they'd simply relied on the district's traditional entrepreneurialism or if change had been mandated from the top down.

LESSONS LEARNED

How transferable is all this experience? For example, how might it inform practice in a school where large numbers of children are struggling and nobody can wait a half-century for things to improve? If the answer isn't to try to transplant specific procedures from one place to another, then what is it? Perhaps, first, that it can be useful to look at one's own reality from a different perspective.

Earlier, for instance, I discussed the theory driving many of today's reforms: that schools are so resistant to change, it has to be imposed even if the consequences are uncertain. An alternative theory is that effective change depends on the willing involvement of those who have to carry it out.

The second premise leads to any number of conclusions: for example, that the most effective institutional change respects or, better yet, embodies an organization's core beliefs and traditions. It also requires trust. Formal leaders provide support for bottom-up reform; they frame the issues, then empower teachers to work them through. Formal and informal leaders collaboratively build structures that provoke good thinking and support good work. Information and decisions are transparent and understandable.

To be certain, the problems some schools confront are so immediate, they require immediate action. More directive, less collaborative change may be unavoidable. But the more sophisticated and subtle the problems, the less likely authoritarian interventions are to produce excellent results. Whatever its short-term needs, a school's long-term growth depends on thoughtful, developmental efforts to build and nurture a culture of learning.

As a colleague once said, the way to solve the problems of a chaotic high school may be to introduce an early childhood program.

CHAPTER 11

WORLD-CLASS LEARNING

The Clinton Goals 2000 initiative said the United States would be first in the world in math and science by the turn of the new century. Implicitly, education was an international race, an idea that for me evokes images of trucks on the interstate: the ones with logos declaring they're carrying "world-class" plumbing supplies or mattresses. What would it mean to be first in the realm of faucets? How would anyone know?

I can understand the appeal of a single global measure of success, perhaps a test that determines who's at the top of an international league table. But the problem of world-class learning begins with the fact that there is no common understanding of what it is. Even assessments like PISA and the Trends in International Math and Science Study (TIMSS) provide just a snapshot of performance that meets a global standard.

To complicate matters, descriptions of "21st-century learning" usually refer to capacities like "critical thinking," and "perseverance," but there's no agreement about what those terms mean, let alone what it might mean to think or persevere at a high international level. Absent an understanding of the goal, it's hard to map out a way to get there.

As the accreditation team said in 2010, these are the kinds of issues that educators have to work out together, step-by-step, figuring out what to do next as they go. Progress can be agonizingly slow. It often opens as many questions as it answers.

In Scarsdale, professional staff started out at a very basic level: "How do we understand what higher-order thinking is?" "How do we teach creativity—or can we teach it at all?" "How can we share our knowledge, get better at cultivating these capacities, and minimize unhelpful variability in our teaching?" There were textbook answers to some of these questions, but to own the ideas and integrate them into daily practice, teachers had to wrestle with them.

Faculty members and administrators discussed what thinking and problem-solving skills are and how they might be developed. Forums included professional development courses, committees, and long-range planning groups, as well as less formal conversations in departments and

across lunch tables. In addition, district leaders had asked the visiting accreditation team to examine how—or whether—thinking skills and problem solving were being integrated into the student experience.

Teachers told the visitors that they'd learned about their colleagues'
teaching by observing, sharing, and borrowing strategies. The visiting
team also saw or heard about the work teachers were doing in their
classes. For example, one group described a final assessment: "Using what
you've learned in 8th grade about geology, physics, and the economics
of Haiti, use affordable materials to construct a model building that will
withstand an earthquake that registers 7.2 on the Richter scale, as well as
its aftershocks. Test your building on an earthquake table."

Meanwhile, Columbia University researchers had observed that
Scarsdale students were involved in higher-order thinking as much as
80% of their class time. But the teachers in the study were volunteers
who had planned their lessons with that specific goal in mind. Many
were working with New York's Lincoln Center Institute, which was
trying to develop a theoretical model for building thinking capacities
through the arts.

In other words, the findings confirmed common sense: Interested
teachers had the knowledge and skill to involve Scarsdale students in
higher-order thinking. But how common was this kind of instruction in
Scarsdale? Could students think any better than before? The research did
not answer those questions.

The accreditation team did note that "open, speculative conversation"
had caused more staff to feel they "owned" the thinking and problem-
solving initiative. "The manifestations . . . are becoming part of the district's culture," the report said, "and there is good reason to believe that
[this] development will continue and deepen. . . . Professional staff appear to understand and agree on the broad scope of the issues that relate
to the redefinition of critical and creative thinking and problem solving
and how they are taught" (Tri-State Consortium, 2010).

Still, faculty and administrators had yet to answer many of the essential questions they'd faced at the very start. In a superintendent's view,
one of the most important was how to honor teachers' individual enterprise and also provide a more consistent learning experience for 4,700
students. For example, could some common principles of teaching become so integral to teachers' thinking that they would come naturally to
bear in daily practice? Might the faculty identify a common line of inquiry
to guide their work?

Some teachers had said they wanted to know specifically what terms
like *critical thinking* and *creative thinking* meant, for example. Others resisted, in part out of a fear of over-regulation. But ambiguity also left room

for desirable variation, they said. Why settle on one definition when unanticipated ones might be good, as well?

Having worked the issues around, participants in a districtwide strategic-planning meeting agreed that more specificity could help progress, although it was important to leave space for alternative views. This seemingly small shift appeared to signal growing recognition that clarity need not necessarily threaten autonomy, as well as trust that the process of collective inquiry was not a top-down master plan.

The result was a suggestion from high school department leaders: A critical thinker will be able to link knowledge from disciplines; understand, embrace, and be comfortable with ambiguity; recognize that there often is no "final answer"; find and use information to address a specific challenge or complex question; question "facts"; and recognize his or her own bias.

These common reference points helped to focus discussion. They also identified observable evidence of critical thinking. That kind of evidence could help teachers understand how to modify or adapt their teaching. If a student were to demonstrate that she was questioning her own biases, for example, a teacher could try to figure out what had prompted the behavior. Then he'd have a better chance of helping her take a productive next step.

One source of evidence might be a student's written work. When she discussed *The Great Gatsby*, for example, did she see beneath Daisy's glamour and ennui to the beguiling, narcissistic, and ultimately weak person inside? Could she distinguish between the narrator's viewpoint and her own opinions or prejudgments? The answers would inform the way the teacher next approached her.

Classroom observation also could be a source of evidence. How did students react in a discussion or debate? Could they explain their thinking or show that they saw a different point of view? Could they change their minds? Supported by rubrics and formal protocols, the observations also could be a form of assessment.

WHAT IS "WORLD CLASS"?

As the accreditation team had said, these efforts to offer a 21st-century education had produced meaningful, if incremental, changes in school programs and practice. Still, they had not answered the questions of whether student work met a high global standard or of how to help students produce work of that quality. Since standardized tests shed little light on the subject, those questions ideally would have been a focus of government interest and funding.

Any number of education ministries overseas wanted to promote aspects of learning that standardized tests assess poorly, if at all. Singapore was trying to move beyond its traditional, exam-oriented curriculum. Four Shanghai educators had spent 5 months in Scarsdale, trying to see how America developed critical and creative thinkers.

Following the 2008 election, it briefly had seemed as if USED also might start to rethink its approach to assessment. Officials began to say their main objective was not so much to hold schools accountable for students' performance as to develop information to help educators teach better. One might have expected that interest to translate into a search for significantly better measures.

Nonetheless, federal policies continued to emphasize testing for accountability. States went on using the same kinds of tests they'd used for years. As we've learned, these exams measured what they measured reliably and consistently. They also had technical limitations and, more important, did not measure much of the learning that was most meaningful. They said nothing about whether performance met a high global standard or how schools helped students produce work at that level.

A second kind of assessment—AP tests and the International Baccalaureate exams, for example—wasn't as statistically valid and reliable as standardized tests. Nonetheless, it was generally understood to be a rigorous measure of more complex, significant learning. Teams of experts developed questions; trained raters evaluated the responses. As we've seen from Scarsdale's AT experience, however, these kinds of measures could limit innovation and responsiveness to student interests, and promote a test-prep mentality. They offered little intelligence about what learning looks like at a global level, either.

To obtain textured information about their students' learning, teachers still had to rely on locally developed measures: tests, papers, projects, oral exams. They could exercise judgment about what to ask and about what constituted a good answer. Of course, the quality of questions and scoring depended on the teacher or teachers. Results weren't as consistently reliable as they were on a standardized test, but then an instructor wasn't bound to downgrade the child who said a fictional character was "disappointed" instead of "sad"—the "correct" response to a question on a recent New York State language arts test.

Federal and state policies emphasized standardized tests, recognized AP and similar exams, and for practical purposes discounted the value of local measures. Unfortunately, no standardized measure simultaneously provided useful, timely information about advanced learning, yielded results that were statistically reliable and valid, and was inexpensive enough for widespread administration. It was unclear whether any ever would. Nonetheless, understanding the limits of what existed, federal officials decided to create a new generation of super-tests.

In 2011, USED awarded $360 million of Race to the Top money to two groups of states. One is called the Smarter Balanced Assessment Consortium (SBAC). The second is the Partnership for Assessment of Readiness for College and Careers (PARCC). The plan was to develop computerized tests that included both standardized, short-answer items and "performance" questions that would evaluate capacities such as the ability to read and write complex text, to complete experiments and research projects, and to work with digital media.

Short-answer items (multiple choice, fill-in-the-blanks) certainly could be better than those on many state exams today. SBAC's plan, consequently, was to introduce state-of-the-art "adaptive" testing. If a child missed a question on fractions, for example, a computer program would send him to related items that would explore where he went off track. Did he fail to understand a basic concept or just make a computational error? A child who got the original question right would be directed to other items.

But how much better would the questions actually be? I asked a senior fellow at the American Institutes for Research (AIR), one of the world's largest not-for-profit behavioral and social science research organizations, to describe the "leading-edge" kinds of short-answer items he was developing. Although they were superior to traditional fill-in-the-bubble responses, the questions still assessed a limited amount of learning at a fairly basic level: Can the test-taker distinguish between the idea of two-thirds and the idea of three-quarters?

Originally, there was talk about the performance portions of SBAC and PARCC assessments including open-ended responses similar to the essays on AP exams. Or about their using computer simulations (a virtual wetland that would respond differently to different types of runoff, for example). Since the tests were supposed to assess students' readiness for careers, as well as college, some questions were likely to be more practical, less theoretical or academic. Human graders would have to rate more-complex responses.

The hope was that these new tests would involve students with engaging tasks and measure a wider range of skills and knowledge than before. Despite early optimism, however, the initiatives ran into a range of practical difficulties.

Early on, for instance, there was discussion about introducing more pre- and post-tests to measure students' growth. There was also interest in evaluating how well they could analyze and perform complex tasks in real time, over a period of days or weeks. Theoretically, the measure—perhaps a computer simulation like the one I described above—would be integrated completely into what they were learning in class. It would be assessment *as* instruction, indistinguishable from the lessons.

The concept was as old as formal education. Good teachers have always observed what their pupils were learning and evaluated their progress in order to determine next steps. What was new was the idea that a state education department would prescribe learning activities for all children in all schools on a specific schedule. The prospect led back to the concern about how much education should conform to a single (in this case, externally imposed) template for every student in a state, instead of growing organically from local priorities and student needs.

In the end, many of the early plans were scaled back, in part because of the high cost of test administration and of grading the answers to complex problems. SBAC's computerization plans ran up against the reality that many schools lacked the hardware to test large numbers of children at a single time. There were also renewed concerns about whether the intellectual capital and time involved in giving multiple tests would produce commensurate benefit. How often does every child in America have to take standardized exams in order to be well prepared for college and career? How many students would be at least as well educated if they and their teachers were doing other things?

PARCC and SBAC exams were field tested in 2014, with the final products due in 2015. Both included some performance-based questions and a majority of multiple-choice items. Both offered a mid-year formative assessment as well as a year-end summative test. Both were aligned with the new Common Core curriculum and were therefore harder than many existing state exams. PARCC made less use of computers than SBAC but did employ "evidence-centered design" principles, with questions that required students to use data and other evidence to reason toward conclusions.

Nonetheless, neither consortium had taken a quantum leap forward, as some had said they would. The new tests would be incrementally better versions of what already existed. They would not measure many of the advanced abilities that presumably are the goal of a world-class education in the 21st century. Predictably, state officials would claim they were excellent and essential to certify students' achievement. In the real world, over-reliance on standardized measures would continue to undermine true excellence.

THE ROAD NOT TAKEN—AUTHENTIC ASSESSMENT

To imagine one alternative reality, let's back up to the early 1980s when many educators were less concerned about producing good test-takers than about lifelong learning. They wanted to evaluate pupils' growth, but they also wanted to use assessment to motivate students and to draw out teachers' creativity. Many were determined not to repeat the mistakes of the 1960s and 1970s, when efforts to engage students too often led to lower expectations and diluted academic content.

Forward-thinking reformers, typified by Theodore Sizer's Coalition of Essential Schools, sought to identify a limited number of clear learning objectives. High-quality local assessments would determine how well students were meeting these objectives and where they needed help. Better information would enable teachers to improve their students' learning (Coalition of Essential Schools, 2015).

Ideally, the assessments would include interesting problems that mimicked real-world tasks: "Write a letter to your school principal to advocate for an important change in school policy." Better yet, a group of 6th-graders might study the health of a local pond. They could conduct research, write a report, and perhaps present a case for its protection to local environmental and zoning boards. The presentation might result in regulatory change. That would really be an authentic assessment.

Teachers would establish common criteria to judge students' work. They'd assess the work together to make ratings consistent. The collaboration also would deepen their understanding of the curriculum and sharpen their insight into what quality performance was. The best assessments would be valid and reliable enough from a practical, if not statistical, standpoint, and they would measure meaningful learning. Students would find them motivating, historically not a characteristic of standardized testing in the United States.

Even some members of the standardized testing establishment abroad recognize the value of more engaging assessments, at least to judge from the reaction of experts at the University of Cambridge in England. During a visit to see experts at the Cambridge International Examinations headquarters, I traced the trajectory of the accountability movement for my hosts. "At home," I tried to explain, "we've been trying to keep perspective, but it hasn't been easy. We want our teachers to have latitude to innovate; we don't want them to focus on prepping kids for exams."

That would be terrible, replied a woman who worked at the heart of the testing establishment in a nation Americans may associate with rigid exam requirements and test prep. In the ensuing conversation, another asked whether the two of them could visit Scarsdale. They wanted to see how students would react to their questions. As one said, if the people who take a test are not interested in the problems, they are less likely to do very well on them.

But back in the United States, the imperatives of high-stakes standardized testing had displaced efforts to develop authentic assessments in the 1990s. Focusing on accountability, federal and state governments channeled funding into new exams that would look a lot like the old ones. School districts were hard pressed just to keep up with state demands. Few districts had the time or energy, let alone the money, to develop measures of their own.

TOWARD A HIGH INTERNATIONAL STANDARD

In schools that want to provide a world-class education, curriculum, instruction, and measurement are integrated, equal parts of a whole. Assessment informs and does not drive instruction. It consists of a balance between standardized testing and other kinds of measures.

In addition, educators must understand what a global standard is and how the world's strongest schools help students reach it. Currently, assessments like PISA and TIMSS are today's best hope of finding answers. According to these measures, the United States typically ranks in the middle to lower half of developed nations. There is debate about the significance of these results, but even if we assume they are highly meaningful, they're like thermometer readings: They identify a condition at a moment.

Students in Finland have been top performers on PISA's test of science reasoning. One can obtain scores of those who have taken the exam and see the questions they were asked. But that doesn't say much about what they are learning when they are in school, or about how schools get them to learn it.

Teachers need to know more about what global-standard thinking, writing, and problem solving look like on a day-to-day basis. They need textured evidence of the work that average and stronger students actually do in class. They also need to understand why teachers overseas believe that work is of high quality, as well as what their curriculums and teaching methods are. Currently, there's no way to do that.

The Council of Chief State School Officers is developing a resource bank called Ed Steps to rate student papers and problem-solving exercises on a scale that ranges from "novice" to "expert." Teachers will be able to use the scale to benchmark their own pupils' performance. However, the work samples won't be anchored to an international standard, and there won't be a way to tell how schools get students to produce quality work.

Scarsdale invited a small group of high-performing schools and partner universities in high-performing Australia, Canada, Finland, Shanghai, and Singapore to form a Global Learning Alliance that would try to shed light on answers to these questions. Researchers looked at:

- Assignments and questions students encounter in these schools
- Curriculum guides, texts, and other teaching materials
- Student work (written papers, projects, videos or podcasts, presentations, performances such as science fairs or math contests)
- Standards, rubrics, and protocols teachers use to evaluate the work

What work did teachers in the different countries view as typical and as exemplary? Did some aspects of excellent performance seem to be universal? Did some kinds of assignments naturally elicit exemplary work? (For example, were some kinds of questions more likely than others to lead pupils to analyze problems in an informed way?) Were some curriculums or teaching methods especially effective? Why?

Early results suggested that differences among nations might be more stylistic than qualitative. For example, "best work" in the United States was a project that examined water rights in the Colorado River basin; in Australia, it was a more traditional essay on U.S. politics and economics during the 1920s and 1930s. Relative to typical American curriculums, Australia's appeared to take a somewhat leftist political perspective. But the quality of the work itself wasn't remarkably different from that done by able students in a strong U.S. high school.

At the same time, the fact that student work is less traditional does not necessarily mean it is developing or assessing higher-order capacities. For example, one collaborative student project overseas ended in an authentic product: an illustrated guidebook for a local nature preserve. Essentially, the book was a primer in plant and animal identification, with text that was mostly a description of what a visitor would see in the preserve. It didn't provoke critical or creative thinking. Students very probably employed higher-order skills to *produce* it, but there was no way to tell whether that was a conscious goal of the project.

The research suggested that certain variables may be unrelated to the quality of students' thinking skills, at least in Alliance schools. Students in Finland go to school 4 to 7 hours a day, 190 days a year; in Shanghai, the day is 8 to 9 hours long, 230 days a year. In the Finnish schools that were part of the study, unions are relatively strong. They are not a significant force in the Global Alliance schools in Australia or Singapore.

The high-performing schools in the Alliance do share certain characteristics. All of them have a clear sense of mission that includes a commitment to teaching global capacities (however they define that term), an emphasis on critical thinking and nonstandard problem solving, and a determination to foster a spirit of service and contribution. They hire top graduates as teachers. Professional development is strong and comprehensive. Parents are engaged in their children's learning. The schools participate in international student and teacher exchanges, and they involve their students in a variety of service activities.

To obtain the greatest benefit from the Alliance, teachers in the member schools will need to communicate directly with their international counterparts both live and virtually. One result, a technology-based international learning community, may be the ultimate embodiment of the maxim that conversation among teachers—a dialogue that expands perspectives and understanding—is the oxygen that feeds meaningful educational change.

Whether Alliance schools will be able to translate their future discussions systematically into practice will depend on whether they can extract transferable lessons from their collective research. That may not be easy. Some of what they have learned so far is consistent with existing research: Critical and creative thinking are not discrete and do not occur in isolation. They transcend organizational and disciplinary boundaries. That makes them hard to teach in any organized, systematic way.

More encouraging, these capacities do appear to be associated with activities where people:

- Construct their own understanding and knowledge
- Conduct authentic research and discover for themselves
- Collaborate
- Participate in Socratic dialogue
- Undertake authentic projects and demonstrate learning in authentic settings
- Reflect on their own learning

Furthermore, teachers seem more apt to promote critical and creative thinking when they:

- Work collaboratively in established cultures of reflective practice
- Identify these objectives as priorities and make them clear to students

- Participate in lesson study and other collaborative practices
- Focus on real-world problem solving and authentic project-based learning
- Build large, essential concepts from one grade to the next, then tie those "big ideas" to quality assessments (often inquiry-driven and real-world, project-based)

Is there a way to connect any of these strategies with better outcomes? Are some more productive than others? How *can* 21st-century schools measure progress against a high global benchmark? Those kinds of questions could constitute an agenda for a decade. They do not—or at least they should not—concern only a small group of high-performing schools.

They are relevant to any school seeking to offer an education for the 2000s. Enlightened federal and state policy would support this kind of research financially, disseminate the results, and create networks of schools and universities to translate the results into practice. The work is labor-intensive, and a single school or small group of schools can do it only on the margins, after teachers have taught their classes and corrected their papers. It's hard enough to find time and space for professional exchanges within a single school, let alone for more theoretical inquiry involving teachers from schools around the globe.

These questions are especially important to the education of young people in less favored communities, who depend especially on their schools to help them. Teachers in these schools simultaneously have to develop students' fundamental skills, stretch their imaginations, *and* ignite their interest in learning. They have to be particularly interested in the nature of critical or innovative thinking: what those capacities mean and what they look like. How can teachers help children acquire them? What activities (mentoring and coaching, collaboration such as lesson study) are most likely to build professional capacity to do this important work?

In the end, a discussion of assessment leads to essential questions about the kind of education that will emerge after today's economic harrowing and Race to the Top's distorted use of test scores. No reputable educator objects to responsible measurement, but the 20th-century industrial impulse to quantify and standardize is undermining world-class education in the 21st. Schools that meet a high international standard cannot afford to let assessment drive instruction. It must be a tool to help teachers improve their practice and change lives.

CHAPTER 12

BEYOND CORPORATE EDUCATION

Critics of corporate reform have a responsibility to offer positive alternatives to the status quo. The challenge they face, the challenge of providing a true education for tomorrow, is to conserve the best of the past while also embracing promising change. But what is worth preserving? And what is most promising?

What is worth preserving? The objectives of a classic liberal education: fostering good thinkers, problem-solvers, self-realized people. The humanity of the student–teacher encounter. Interactions through which students learn from one another. Opportunities to become involved with rich and challenging educational content.

What's promising? Online learning at any hour, often with the help of virtual networks of people of all ages. Experiences that cut across disciplinary boundaries, as well as those that blend academics and the real world. To remain relevant in the 2000s, some experts say, schools have to do the things technology cannot.

Samples of 21st-century practices exist in many places, but a fully realized education for the year 2030 or 2040 doesn't. Innovation appears in pockets: single classrooms, special programs, alternative schools. It's less likely to be imbedded in whole schools or school districts.

The familiar designs of the 19th century—the factory-style building, the academic subjects, course credits—have remarkable staying power. Often, today's reforms reinforce these well-worn structures; many charter schools are highly traditional, for instance.

Meanwhile, schools and teachers are inventing education for tomorrow as they go, winnowing promising practices from the chaff of novelty. Nobody knows what doors technology will open or which corridors will turn out to be dead ends.

Given these realities, what does 21st-century education look like?

THE 21ST-CENTURY SCHOOL

Curriculum and Thinking Skills

At a time when the universe of information is both immense and instantly retrievable, skills and content acquisition are increasingly means, not ends. Students in 21st-century schools still master basic skills and significant content. But from its earliest years, their education cultivates the higher-order abilities of analysis, evaluation, and creativity.

We know we can elicit critical thinking by pushing people to examine and defend ideas. Methods like the Harkness table or Socratic seminars involve students with significant texts and subject their ideas to close analysis. Curriculums like Singapore math encourage them to question, analyze, and search for alternative solutions. Good writing instruction forces students to develop and clarify their thoughts.

Training people to be creative is even more difficult than enabling them to think critically. The very idea may be oxymoronic. Can creativity be taught or is it only possible to create conditions that favor it? How much is it innate and how much the product of an environment? We are unsure. In the end, the best that schools may be able to do to promote creativity is to provide a "Goldilocks" environment that creates intellectual disequilibrium without disabling stress.

Some theorists say critical and/or creative thinking can be taught by immersing young children in the arts. Others try to isolate and teach specific dimensions of thinking, like imagination, or they focus on developing certain behaviors, like making connections. Nobody understands whether learning to identify patterns or developing other isolated intellectual skills actually enhances complex thinking. We can't even be confident that a relatively simple physical activity like practicing returns on a tennis court will translate into expert play.

Traditional curriculums assume that analytical thinking develops naturally in the process of studying subjects like math. They also tend to assume that creativity is the domain of the arts. Researchers are coming to realize that these different ways of thinking are interconnected and that they often connect with physical activity as well.

To build a dry stone wall, for example, a mason has to fit different shapes and pieces into a whole. The work follows conventions (lay stones lengthwise, but periodically anchor them crosswise; avoid the vertical seams called "runs"). It is simultaneously an original problem-solving exercise. The builder may have to settle a rounded conglomerate that doesn't want to be stable, while making sure the whole wall stays aligned and strong.

Reason and physical action can disconnect when you are building a wall, so that your mind runs free to other matters. As that happens, intuitive intelligence, a kind of developed instinct, kicks in and guides your physical actions. This kind of creativity can produce an original aesthetic statement, a structure that's elegant, not just functional. It also might define surrounding space in unexpected and pleasing ways. Artist Andy Goldsworthy's fieldstone walls are examples.

An intriguing question for 21st-century schools is how to develop academic analogues to stone wall building. How can they make learning into an engaging puzzle that motivates the student and ends in satisfaction? One possible lead is the work Joseph Renzulli has done at the University of Connecticut's National Center for Gifted Education.

Renzulli asks teachers to expose students to disciplines, topics, occupations, and hobbies they wouldn't usually find in a school curriculum. Their personal interests lead them to activities that can develop thinking and learning skills. After being introduced to an urban-planning problem, for example, a youngster could do advanced reading, plan, and experiment with alternative solutions. She then could work with a mentor on a self-selected topic that required more advanced knowledge. She ultimately might demonstrate her mastery by making a presentation to a civic organization or planning commission, similar to the one I mentioned earlier.

As the example suggests, a starting point for this sort of self-initiated inquiry is a repertoire of topics, activities, or opportunities that both reflect important ideas and promise to hook kids. In Scarsdale, student-initiated research starts in the earliest grades and culminates in the self-selected capstone project. By high school, opportunities become more specialized. Students can pursue their questions in courses like Science Research. Other classes also have significant inquiry research extensions.

Common features of these experiences include the fact that students are active explorers who uncover new information in an area of personal interest. They develop new insights by interacting with a teacher, other expert adults, and/or other students. They apply their knowledge in the real world—perhaps through a presentation to a group of people who care about the quality of the result. Often these experiences also reflect a teacher's or mentor's personal influence.

At best, this kind of learning helps students develop capacities that college teachers and many employers seek in their pupils and employees, qualities like perseverance, self-discipline, and a deep interest in learning. As a professor at Brown University told me, "I want the kid who can keep going despite the obstacles, the one with a passion to know." Some college teachers say that beyond a few big ideas, they don't really care what their students remember from high school. "I'd rather they learn the material my way anyhow," is a typical comment.

Curriculum and Globalism

To help students become effective participants in an interdependent world, 21st-century schools also develop "global consciousness," the ability to see through others' eyes, to value people's differences as well as their commonalities, and to act out of a sense of personal and social responsibility.

To understand how Western culture and perspectives relate to others, 21st-century students have to grapple with cross-disciplinary issues like regional conflict or sustainability, an international concern that involves demographics, natural resources, agronomy, politics, and economics. Their studies may thread through the curriculum, beginning in kindergarten. Alternatively or additionally, they may meet a global studies requirement by choosing from a graduated menu of experiences over 13 years.

Schools of the 21st century also recognize the importance of personal experience in developing cross-cultural understanding. By the time they graduate, therefore, students will have lived with a family or worked on projects elsewhere. To be certain, everyone won't be able to go to Ghana to distribute mosquito netting. However, "another culture" may exist only a few miles or a few blocks away from home. It also should be possible to teleconference or to collaborate online with students overseas, to research and propose solutions to a problem like disease in West Africa, for example.

Curriculum and Connections

Implicit in global problem solving is the idea of finding connections among places, people, and ideas. For many young people, however, much of what goes on in school seems unrelated to anything meaningful. It remains inert and uninviting. They don't commit themselves to it. They learn little from it.

Properly chosen, thorny real-world issues and real-world connections invite student engagement. For example, an acquaintance who taught in New York City once told me about his attempts to help disaffected 10th-graders learn to read. The only middle ground between what interested them and what he had to teach was the subway system. So he ended up using subway maps to get them to read.

The particular example may seem unrelated to teaching and learning in other kinds of communities, ones where more-compliant children make more-cooperative scholars. The connecting thread is the importance of helping young people see connections. People make meaning of new knowledge by seeing how it relates to knowledge they already have, to other knowledge, and to things that matter to them.

Curriculum and Structure

The 20th-century curriculum is a significant obstacle to cross-disciplinary learning and the study of real-world problems. It is based on the 19th-century structure of academic subjects that was invented to categorize knowledge and make it manageable. (The reason we have a field called chemistry is that it is a way to order and understand what had become an overwhelming amount of related information.)

Other conventions grew up to reinforce the subject divisions. Academic departments institutionalized the disciplinary silos. Teacher education and certification, state course requirements, and tests reinforced the disciplines. The "Carnegie Unit" (in which a certain amount of learning is supposed to equal a certain number of class hours, which equal so many credits) cemented the structure in place. More on that shortly. Now, the new Common Core buttresses the entire edifice.

The mass of all these structures means that relatively few youngsters in the United States ever get involved with project-based learning like High Tech High School's research in San Diego Bay. If they do original research—the kind of work colleges and many jobs require—it's normally in addition to five or six other, required courses. Real-world links to unlike peoples and cultures tend to occur through isolated field trips or through exchange programs involving relatively few students, not in academic classes.

Cross-disciplinary, research-based programs are also apt to run afoul of the daily schedule. For instance, the Cambridge International Examinations program offers a Global Issues course in the junior year of high school that features a 2-hour interdisciplinary seminar on world problems. Students write a qualifying paper in preparation for senior year, when they do extended research on a topic of their choice, meet with their teacher in Oxford-style tutorials, and write an in-depth, scholarly thesis. When the day is divided into seven or nine equal periods, most students can never have this kind of experience.

Underlying all of these specific obstacles is the hard fact that schools are collective institutions whose success in meeting many diverse individual needs is necessarily limited. By definition, they have to operate on assumptions about which practices will benefit the largest number of people. If the assumption is that disciplinary learning works best for most, and that it occurs best in brief blocks of time, then there's little flexibility for other approaches.

Exceptions to these rules are not more common for many reasons. Backing for the status quo is strong. There is a legitimate justification for the disciplines. Some teachers believe the traditional, daily 42- or 43- or 45-minute period is ideal for reinforcing the skills they teach. Nobody wants to give up hard-won instructional time.

Nonetheless, new technology and 24-7 learning offer intriguing glimpses into a possible future of less restrictive school parameters. The mechanics of this future are not clear, and the possibilities can raise concerns. For example, will mainstream schools be able to move away from the traditional 6- or 7-hour school day as long as they provide day care for young children, serve as holding facilities for teenagers, and run athletic programs in the late afternoons? Still, the potential is great.

Meanwhile, and depending on their tolerance for innovation, schools can promote less traditional activities in many ways. For example, they can schedule all or part of some days in larger interdisciplinary blocks of time. They can suspend the familiar course grid temporarily, take a day or a week out of the schedule for work on cross-disciplinary problems. They can ask students to make interdisciplinary connections for themselves and to demonstrate their understanding through a paper or oral presentation.

Teaching and Personalization

Recalling his undergraduate years, President James A. Garfield described the ideal college as a log with a master teacher on one end and a student on the other. The metaphor suggested that a real education is personal, a process in which one human being (a teacher) engages another (the student) with questions and ideas at the moment that they will enlarge the student's understanding.

Historically, only the very wealthy could afford an experience that approached this ideal. The closest most Americans would get was mass schooling, whose clumsy mechanics all but precluded the more personal attention available in independent schools, let alone an education tailored to the individual. Today, however, technology makes it possible to think about a kind of learning for the many that was long reserved for the few.

The Scarsdale plan of the 1920s featured individual student contracts, tutorials, and small learning groups. The idea was to break free from what Superintendent Ralph Underwood called the "morass" of mass schooling, but 90 years ago the plan turned out to be too complex to manage. Today's technology will never replace the insight, support, and guidance a skilled teacher can provide, but it can help to give students more personal attention.

Consider what's being called "the flipped classroom," for example. Monday's homework is an on-demand podcast about the origins of the Cold War. On Tuesday, the teacher helps students understand puzzling aspects of what they saw the night before. Small groups consider questions that extend the lesson: "Can we describe the Cold War as a case study in national paranoia?" Meanwhile, the teacher works with a handful of students who are refining essays on the paradoxes of power.

Some corporate education proponents are enthusiastic about technology innovations like this because of their potential to reduce what they call "head count" (a term that, to me, dehumanizingly suggests that people can be culled like cattle). While staffing efficiencies might be a side effect of progressive practice in schools of the 21st century, however, the real promise of technology is its potential to change the dynamic of instruction.

Used judiciously, computer gaming, simulations, Internet access, and other resources turn students into more active learners. When people take more responsibility for their own learning and when learning is a process of exploration and questioning, the teacher's guidance becomes more important, not less. If anyting, he has to be more inventive and responsive to individual differences than before.

Garfield's log was a 19th-century metaphor, assuming in a 19th-century way that a real education occurs through encounters with human greatness: personal brilliance, forceful personality, and other unquantifiable qualities of character. For years, meanwhile, educators have talked about transforming teaching from a process of delivering information into one of questioning, provoking, and mentoring. How do these two concepts connect?

In the real world, where teachers work with 25 or 30 children in an elementary classroom, 125 or more at secondary level, student differences have always outstripped adults' capacity to respond. The promise of technology is not only that it changes pedagogy; it also enables teachers to make the process more personal, more human.

Traditionally, for instance, learning to write was often a process of striving for mechanical accuracy and laboring to copy earlier drafts. Using a computer, young authors constantly can rework sentences, shift paragraphs, and clarify their thinking. By observing this work as it evolves, a teacher has more opportunities to explore students' ideas and "reasons why." In this more collaborative context, each is more likely to see the other as a human being.

In a more reciprocal relationship, one person can still have knowledge and wisdom the other doesn't. But teachers can know and support their students better. Hitherto hidden facets of their personalities should be more available to one another. And where understanding and respect exist, people are less likely to view their interactions in terms of power, and more apt to listen to and learn from one another.

I've been describing mentoring relationships that cause students to invest themselves in learning. I've said that technology can help personalize curriculum and make material more engaging. But the realist in me also recalls that whatever they promise, schools have always managed to find ways to make learning uninteresting and irrelevant.

I remember the teachers who told me, "You won't understand the reasons for this until you get to high school (or college). Just do what you're told." So I performed the mechanics without understanding why they worked or were important, and never got to advanced math. Education was knowledge concealed in a sanctuary behind veils of ascending mastery. Technology won't solve this problem by itself, but it can help teachers humanize their pupils' learning.

To conclude: Technology and economics have transformed fields from business to journalism to medicine. The forms of schooling have stayed relatively constant. I've suggested that this persistence has reflected historical realities: social conservatism and the slow pace at which practice evolves, for instance. In addition, the organization of the school continues to be defined by subject specialization, the daily schedule, and the Carnegie Unit. Schools for tomorrow are struggling to transcend these limitations.

FEDERAL AND STATE GOVERNMENT

Federal and state policies continue to follow century-old paths, hoping somehow to achieve new results. They prescribe standards, curriculum, and tests. They set course and credit requirements. They monitor for compliance and punish noncompliance. Strategies like these reinforce the forms of an education built for the year 1955.

Standards

In the past century, states developed detailed definitions of knowledge and skills that students were to learn in each subject. Now, many of them have signed on to national standards developed by the National Governors Association and the Council of Chief State School Officers. These standards, the Common Core, are generating controversy.

The political right sees the Core as a federal takeover of state and local education. Some on the left think it will discourage school and student innovation. Pragmatists say that even though it is imperfect, it may be better than much of what exists. Their main concern is that the tests and teaching units associated with the Common Core will establish *de facto* a unitary national curriculum subject to the drawbacks associated with AP courses.

An underlying problem is that many of the new standards aren't broad learning goals so much as they are learning objectives: the specifics curriculum builders have in mind when they organize subject matter for instruction. The level of detail is so great, there is no way to keep all—or even most—of it in mind on a daily basis, and it is unwieldy for use in monitoring overall program effectiveness or the progress of numbers of students.

More productive would be to specify and monitor a more economical core of standards: basic skills, big ideas, and thinking capacities. For example: Students should be able to write a grammatically correct paper that evaluates a complex problem. They should be able to use historical evidence to draw meaningful conclusions about current events. They should understand how to use statistics to analyze an unknown.

Standards like these often draw on more than one academic subject. They can help teachers and students understand and concentrate on what's ultimately most important to learn. They are also compact enough for teachers to bear in mind when they approach a week's or a day's lesson planning. They constitute significant performance targets, the sort that matter in the long run.

Curriculum

The basis for granting academic credit in the 20th century was the Carnegie Unit: time served. In the 2000s, credit should reflect demonstrated mastery of certain skills and content, where possible. Time requirements will still be appropriate for other learning. A student may be able to read a critical essay and then write an acceptable paper on *Moby-Dick* in short order. However, the extended process of class discussion cultivates perspective and ways of thinking and is inherently valuable. Students deserve to experience the process.

Which learning should be certified in a more traditional way and which should not? If credit is based on mastery, not time served, will schools need as many teachers as before? Will they reduce staff or recommit "saved" positions to support struggling or advanced students, or to deepen learning for everyone? My inclinations are obvious, but these questions will defy easy resolution, especially in a politicized, low-trust environment.

Enlightened state departments of education also will rework traditional course requirements. Whether a middle school offers an interdisciplinary humanities course or separate English and social studies classes, for example, what matters is that students learn to write an effective paper, to read literature critically, and to understand the interplay of broad historical, economic, political, and cultural forces. Broad ends, more than course titles, will be organizing principles.

Related, in the last years of high school, progressive states will adopt broad college-readiness or career-readiness requirements. Some students will elect a relatively traditional course of study. Others will study a reduced, compact core of disciplinary studies part of the time. The rest of their program will consist of interdisciplinary inquiry, structured fieldwork, and/or research. Either path will involve complex content and high-level thinking.

Teaching

A more open, flexible environment is changing learning and teaching. With online access to the Internet, schools and students are developing real-world, community-based connections both during and outside the school day. As students initiate more of their own learning in networks and as they work collaboratively with others, teaching will come to feature more guiding, mentoring, advising, and tutoring.

Teachers need to be better educated and more skilled than ever. But where will they come from? The conventional wisdom is that poor teaching is largely a result of outmoded tenure laws, ineffective evaluation, and unions that protect incompetents. When I was a beginning administrator, I felt much the same.

I remember the Massachusetts Teachers Association representative who said he'd defend a rock if it belonged to the MTA. The mentality was provocative and insulting. Undeniably, it continues to insulate the unfit, to promote retrograde work rules, and to perpetuate a grudging, lowest–common–denominator work ethic. To remain relevant and viable, teachers' organizations have to move beyond 20th-century trade unionism and promote a more progressive, professional agenda.

Still, there's no evidence that students in states without tenure and unions are any better educated than those in states with them; if anything, the reverse may be true. If, as I've argued, the real challenge is to raise the average quality of teaching across the board, a first question is how to recruit candidates whose academic background is as strong as those of applicants selected for Teach for America (the project that attracts promising graduates from selective colleges—and then, unfortunately, watches the large majority walk away from the classroom after a year or two).

World leader Finland once had quality problems similar to America's, but its situation has improved markedly. Today, only eight Finnish universities educate teachers. Their curriculums are similar. Professors all have doctorates. In contrast, New York City alone has almost 70 colleges and universities. Programs can differ significantly. Professors' credentials vary, and they may be full-time employees or part-time adjuncts.

State governments in the United States can adopt policies aimed at improving teacher preparation. One strategy would be to close a large number of existing teacher education programs so that competition for places would improve the quality of the pool. However, so many teachers leave the field each year that a shrunken supply would not nearly meet the demand. The alternatives are to go on with business more or less as usual, or to create incentives that will attract and keep more highly qualified people.

The general quality of the teaching force certainly will not improve if compensation becomes even less attractive, if there's little inservice support, and if the main focus of the work is prepping children for exams. Government that is serious about improving education will find ways to improve salaries and benefits. It will promote learning communities that include networks of schools, universities, and other institutions. It also will find ways to entrust and empower teachers and to give them significant control over their practice.

Assessment

Current federal and state policies make government responsible for holding every principal and teacher personally accountable for the achievement of every single child. The approach is inelegant, inefficient, and needlessly intrusive. A rational plan would be to limit testing for accountability to a bare minimum and to redirect funds to help needy districts and schools improve teaching and learning.

Administering, reading, grading, certifying, and processing individual tests in multiple subjects at multiple grades costs millions of dollars each year. Once a month, all 700-some districts in New York upload masses of data on every individual student and teacher in the state. The cost to any single district of preparing, verifying, and processing this amount of detailed information is huge. And the number of tests continues to grow.

This system produces volumes of data that aren't essential to intelligent policy. They are not necessary for systems monitoring. Trying to control for quality at this micro level is inefficient. Washington and state capitals should be concerned with whether districts and subgroups are progressing toward core learning goals. They don't have to spend precious resources tracking every individual child's scores each year when far less intrusive sampling techniques can assess growth, as the NAEP does.

A more effective monitoring program also will recognize objective differences among the things it monitors. That is what high-performing nations around the world do. Some of America's schools already prepare students well for college and careers. Some show special promise. Others are clearly foundering and need help. Some should close. It is illogical and a waste of resources to treat them the same when they are not. Schools that demonstrate their effectiveness or special promise merit greater freedom. Greater freedom will promote innovation, which will help still more schools improve.

Also, it's time to recognize that while mass testing has its uses, the value of standardized measurement is limited. The two new national assessment consortiums will produce better tests, but how soon will a computer be able to evaluate responses to questions such as "Discuss the nature of evil in *Moby-Dick*" or "Determine who should have water rights to the Colorado River?" For the foreseeable future, human judgment will remain the best measure of important student learning and effective instruction.

Governments could be funding efforts to develop exemplary assessments that embrace the strengths of human judgment: papers, oral exams, and portfolios. They could offer technical assistance to districts or consortiums that build those assessments. They could support teams of school and university teachers who would help validate the measures. And they could help teachers to become more knowledgeable about using assessment to improve learning—the most important goal of education measurement.

RESTORING BALANCE IN GOVERNANCE

Over the past 3 decades, a unique confluence of economic, demographic, and social forces has skewed the relationship among federal, state, and local decisionmakers. In the process, local educators—the solution to the schools' problems—have been disenfranchised. The disequilibrium is destructive; the entire system's success depends on each level's respecting its own capacities and limitations, as well as the others'. A better balance is essential.

Effective policy sets broad goals, capitalizes on strength, and monitors selectively. It doesn't try to control details. To create change that is both lasting and effective, our federal and state governments must, or course, exercise authority. More important, they must educate, collaborate, and lead through wisdom. Absent a climate that nourishes local initiative and creativity, America's schools will continue to prepare graduates for the 1900s.

CHAPTER 13

STOP THE MADNESS

What is the future of public education? Technology will be a source of significant change, but other forces will tend to conserve familiar forms. Faith in quantification isn't going away, so metrics and accountability are with us for good. Charters and vouchers will continue to influence the political structure of schooling, if not the day-to-day character of teaching and learning.

The big business/government/media alliance will have unusual staying power, but it will be years before anyone can really evaluate corporate reform's legacy. Whatever the outcome, it won't produce "break the mold" schools for the 21st century. Efforts to quantify and systematize, to promote competition and contain cost, are not substitutes for a positive vision of education. A strategy of control and audit doesn't liberate talent or foster creativity.

As a practical matter, many school practices will continue to follow the opinion of a public that is cautious about change. A common view holds that education in 1975 or even 1955 was very probably better than it is now. Most people have trouble imagining anything very different, and there are few concrete models of what it might look like. So many think that tomorrow's students need to go forward to something that looks considerably like the past.

With so many conservative forces at work, it's unlikely that all students will reach the same high 21st-century standards in any near future. When an achievement gap still exists down the road, we can anticipate a return engagement with the dilemma of equity and excellence. We likely will revisit the idea that students with different abilities should be educated differently. Already we can hear talk about early tracking, vocational training, and apprenticeship, similar to that in the German system.

The one truly new element in this mix is technological innovation. Its ultimate impact is far from clear. Arguably, for instance, it may be working changes similar to those that transformed medicine during the last half of the 20th century. Health care has become far more technically sophisticated. But medical management and practice are also more specialized and mechanistic, and often less sensitive to the human being who is the patient.

Although technology is more likely to produce evolutionary change than revolution, it doesn't take a large leap to imagine "classrooms of tomorrow" where 40 or 50 small bodies sit alone together, interacting with machines and a teaching aide or two. Possibly, as one futurist suggests, tiny electronic companions will lodge perpetually in their ears, whispering tutorial assistance and other advice. It will be more efficient—and cheaper, too—the dream of some corporate reformers.

Meanwhile, the Great Recession encouraged a perverse politics of self-cannibalization. No new taxes, regardless of need or long-term value; layoffs and program reductions even if they degraded quality; bitter attacks on salaries and benefits that were already inadequate; salary caps that drove school leaders out of the market. As we divided on ourselves, the immediate victims were children. Ultimately, most Americans stood to lose.

In sum, it is not irrational to picture a future of two school systems that are even less equal than today's. One offers a real education. It includes independent schools, some charter schools, and a handful of public schools that have managed to cling to some level of quality. It serves a small group of the affluent and those fortunate enough to win scholarships that give them access to the world of the wealthy.

Everyone else gets "education lite," a meager, mediocre experience. It relies heavily on technology and fewer teachers. Their pay is modest, their benefits lean. The work is heavily standardized and routine; much of it can be done by aides. These shortcomings do not truly matter, though, because much of what school does is to walk children through computer exercises and have them take tests. There is not a lot of depth or humanity in learning.

This dystopian vision may not become reality. Economic stresses may ease before political posturing, self-deception, and regressive policies create a disaster that literally will take decades to repair. Technology may carry us into a brighter future. But regardless, public schooling seems likely for the near future to remain in thrall to the distorted narrative of institutional collapse and salvation by metrics, accountability, and choice.

THE BURDEN OF REFORM

In a strange way, it would be easier if advocates of today's corporate reform policies were all cynically scapegoating schools, cutting costs without thinking about long-term social consequences, or consciously trying to destroy public education. In fact, many of them are decent people with honorable motives, which is almost as disheartening. It would seem that reasoned discussion could have brought people of different persuasions closer together.

Instead, good intentions continue to translate into questionable practice. As I write, educators across New York State are obsessing over the excruciating detail of the performance evaluation scheme I described earlier. They are completing local plans by filling in an online template that consists of multiple-choice items and predetermined short answers. The work consumes immense time and energy. Few think it will help in any significant way.

The experience is more than a little disorienting. For example, one of the more accessible "tips" for compliance enjoins the reader to "see Guidance D22 and E6 and E7 for a list of control variables that may be used for this subcomponent [of the evaluation protocol]." The aforesaid "variables" may be used variously to allocate performance rating points in the required "growth or local measures" (New York State Education Department, 2012).

If the previous paragraph delivered you into catatonia, not to worry. It will pass. For those directly involved, however, the exercise is bewildering in the original sense of the word: It causes one to feel lost in a wilderness. Why try to make statistically insignificant distinctions among different people? Why mandate the use of rigid scoring formulas that cannot possibly anticipate the variety of real situations that affect performance? Why insist on this whole misguided effort to begin with?

To add to the frustration, many school districts abandoned systems like this years ago precisely because of the concerns I've described. They did use common performance standards and tried to be consistent in applying them. But they recognized that some of the best and worst teaching reflects human idiosyncrasy and that it defies precise mathematical description. They were concerned with standardized test results but did not translate students' scores ineluctably into teacher rankings. In short, they understood that meaningful evaluation reflects sound human judgment.

This is just one example of the kind of enforced activity that occupies front-line educators in the era of corporate reform. Especially disheartening is the amount of time it takes when it is so disconnected from work that actually might improve learning.

At the risk of being overly autobiographical: I meet with my Board of Education or its officers at least 200 hours a year. In one year alone, we introduced a new public information plan and started a private foundation to supplement school funding. We spent hundreds of hours developing, proposing, and publicly justifying a $140 million budget.

I visited schools and classrooms and took part in discussions about interdisciplinary courses, the high school schedule and credit requirements, and building renovation plans.

I talked at length with parent and teacher representatives about the tensions in their relationship, their respective concerns about one another, and a cooperative effort to develop protocols to promote productive relations.

Those are just some activities that were relatively predictable parts of the annual cycle. Then there was the unforeseeable. We lost a student in a tragic accident. We parted company with a veteran staff member who would have done fine on the state's 100-point scale, but who was arrested for illegal behavior outside of school. A hurricane destroyed school infrastructure and left the community without electrical power for a week.

The point is not that school superintendents are overworked or that others should feel sorry for us. Rather, it is that "keeping school," regular program concerns, and the unforeseen consume immense energy. Efforts to introduce more significant change—global benchmarking, initiating a Center for Innovation for education redesign, developing measures of thinking and problem-solving skills—are in addition. On top of all that are the requirements that cascade down from above.

Life isn't that different for teachers. In other words, everyone has plenty to do before embarking on tasks that Washington or Albany thinks he or she should be performing. In a better world, government would understand this and interject itself respectfully, selectively, and only where absolutely necessary. In this one, our friends know what's best for us, and they are determined to see that we benefit from their wisdom.

A DYSFUNCTIONAL SYSTEM

For years, I attended meetings with State Education Commissioner Mills, other education department officials, and members of the Board of Regents. From time to time, I would sense that we were about to communicate. Periodically, one of them would acknowledge that the state's initiatives didn't always make sense to a local point of view, and he or she would express an interest in helping.

For the most part, however, the authorities knew where they were headed and were not going to alter course. After a while, I realized that our exchanges were destined to be one-way, circular, and consistently frustrating, and they made me crazy, so I pretty much withdrew. It made more sense to minimize the damage and try to focus on the positive at home.

Commissioner Mills resigned in 2009. His replacement was David Steiner, dean of the School of Education at Hunter College. Mills had taught at New York City's private Dalton School for 2 years before he became a state-level bureaucrat; Steiner was raised in England, attended Oxford, and had no experience as a schoolteacher or administrator. Nonetheless, he was bright and steeped in the humanities, and I had real hope for him.

Whatever I anticipated, state policy in the two administrations turned out to be remarkably consistent. The tone was familiar, too. Shortly after Steiner's appointment, a high-ranking official came to a regional meeting of educators and responded to concerns about one-size-fits-all policies by observing that children were drowning, and he didn't have time for debates.

Having endured budget and staffing cuts for years, and suffering further reductions because of the Great Recession, SED applied for federal Race to the Top funding in 2010. To qualify, the department had to show it had local support. Under a tight deadline, officials told the locals to sign on to the department's application and trust it to work out the specifics in the future. Suddenly, Albany was all about collaboration and cooperation as it actively lobbied the state's 700-some school districts for help.

I wrote Steiner, saying I knew he wasn't responsible for history, but longstanding experience with top-down management made it hard to support a proposal with little idea of what it meant. Subsequently, I received, unsolicited, a friendly phone call from Albany describing the value of our close working relationship and expressing hope that Scarsdale would join the cause. The outreach was unique in my 30 years as a superintendent in New York State.

In the end, Scarsdale's Board of Education endorsed the application. The trustees didn't expect to benefit; their idea was that federal money would go to districts that needed it more. When Washington did approve the funding, Albany announced it would mandate more testing and rate teachers according to students' test scores. Over half the $700 million grant ended up going to construct tests and the state data system, not to local schools.

So much for the short and happy life of collaboration. Considering the shortcomings of the commingled federal and state teacher evaluation policy, a handful of colleagues and I approached our elected representatives in Albany and in Washington. We were not there to rehash arguments over testing, we said. We were worried that the scheme would miscategorize teachers, increase negative competition, and further undermine morale.

At the request of our state senator, Suzy Oppenheimer, Commissioner Steiner and Deputy Commissioner John King agreed to meet with me and another superintendent. What I didn't anticipate was that the conversation would start back at the beginning, in 2001: Why did Scarsdale object to state tests? Surely, they must be a trivial concern for us. A bit startled, I took the group on a trip down memory lane, realizing that I was feeling very tired. The main point was that the tests didn't really help us meet higher standards.

After we had traversed this familiar ground for a while, my hosts finally said that the testing was a federal requirement, so Albany could do nothing about it. What was the problem now? I didn't necessarily agree that SED was powerless, but I hadn't come to re-argue the testing issue to begin with. I described my concerns about the new teacher-rating scheme. These elicited talk of confidence intervals and inter-rater reliability, and unsatisfying assurances that there would be room for significant local control.

In the end, I realized, what the meeting had done was to meet the state officials' obligation to a state senator. I left imagining that the two of them saw me and people like me as political irritants with narrow interests. Or maybe, more charitably, they thought we were the sincere, but irrelevant, opposition: dinosaurs lumbering anachronistically through territory they weren't going to revisit. I pictured their mentally contrasting my petty concerns and limited view with their broad perspective and engineering for the future.

For my part, I felt patronized and controlled. I still had no answer to the questions that had troubled me since the Mills years. If a school could show that it did not need regulation, why would the state want to impose regulations that didn't help it and made its work harder? Why not distinguish among objectively different situations? I could only conclude that the Education Department simply didn't want to; it was easier that way.

Steiner left his post abruptly in 2011. King (since departed to serve as an adviser to Secretary of Education Arne Duncan in Washington) was his successor. Masochistically, but by now seeing the quest as weirdly interesting, I invited several other colleagues to discuss Race to the Top with our congresswoman, Nita Lowey. Did Washington really want school districts to be going down a road that wasn't going to help them improve education significantly? She suggested we talk with Merryl Tisch, the chancellor of the Board of Regents.

The chancellor was forthcoming and positive. She felt that I had made a mistake by not coming to her sooner. If she had attended my meeting with Commissioner Steiner, the outcome could have been very different. It all sounded reasonable, and so it was that we and several other superintendents broke bread with the new commissioner a month later. After an extended exchange about slowing implementation of the new, admittedly imperfect, teacher evaluation regulations ("That ship has sailed"), we turned to the main agenda.

It turned out that nothing could be done about our other concerns either. Federal law required state testing; it was "inadvisable" to try to talk with Washington about more efficient, effective approaches. The new teacher evaluation procedures were also law; there would be no point in talking with legislators about enabling districts to use existing systems that worked. Besides, local concerns would disappear once everyone got used to the state's scheme.

I did hear a new rationale for why the State Education Department wouldn't deregulate high-performing districts: Its data collection system was incomplete; until the work was finished, officials had no way to know who truly was successful. "Maybe," I thought in a snarky sort of way, "parents in communities like mine have been misled, and their children are not really going to the colleges they're going to."

Essentially, SED's message was what it was: "Tests and accountability drive teaching. Better tests and better data systems improve accountability. More accountability makes teaching better. Better learning will follow. Do what you're told."

It was not a productive dynamic. It is not how effective systems work.

THE BALANCE OF POWER

To be fair to my Albany friends, superintendents have complained forever about the heavy-handed bureaucrats above them. At the same time, policymakers have long struggled with the effects of local parochialism and politics. Recently, political struggles over bigger and smaller government have enflamed these traditional tensions. The problem calls for a collaborative solution, a cooperative effort to find a more optimal balance of power.

That will not be easy. Everyone shares the very broad goal of meeting new, high expectations for learning, but after that, the way forward is unclear. Philosophical disagreements can be sharp. Everyone is stretched thin. Trust is not deep. Federal and state bureaucracies and local schools have very different cultures, and their priorities are not entirely the same. Resources are limited.

Nonetheless, a more productive solution is imperative. As we've seen, today's graduates are entering a world in which a "career" is increasingly what the word originally meant: a venture that is high-speed, somewhat headlong, and not entirely predictable. To succeed and contribute, they need to think analytically and innovatively, to work both independently and collaboratively, and to be persistent lifelong learners.

So here is the challenge. Schools of the 20th century were not built to help a full range of students achieve these kinds of results. Many schools today are just trying to meet standards for the 1950s. Others are doing what has made them successful already; when they do change, it's in response to external stimuli like the Common Core.

Schools that are interested in real transformation don't know exactly what the end product should look like, and for the most part, they have to try to work out the answers at the margins. Simply running the existing system—managing, teaching, supporting students and parents—consumes immense energy. Budget woes, human problems, and politics claim more time, sidetracking innovation and growth. Government mandates also claim time and draw down emotional resources. There's little left over.

In my part of New York State and doubtless elsewhere, school districts respond to the latest state intervention the way human systems do when they feel attacked: They try to protect themselves. That's why the great leap forward in teacher evaluation will produce somewhat higher state test scores without improving teaching materially.

To complicate matters, the putative partners in the education enterprise have different objectives and perspectives. State and federal departments of education are regulatory agencies that think bureaucratically about managing systems of thousands or even millions of people. In contrast, a local school district is a mix of representative government and the academy, and it is more apt to think in terms of serving the wants and needs of individuals or smaller groups of constituents.

In addition, priorities at each level of governance also reflect the influence of different ideologies, political agendas, and financial interests. Often, these have to do with constituent desires, power, and money. We have special education laws because local school districts never would have funded special education services otherwise. New York's legislature extended the definition of "special needs" to include children's religious and cultural backgrounds because influential religious groups wanted their children to go to school with children from the same groups.

Finally, limited resources make it difficult for anyone to think or act in new ways. In Albany, for example, there is enough federal money to build a data system. But SED doesn't have the staff or funds to do a robust job of building professional capacity in the field. Even if it did, an agency that is primarily about monitoring and compliance would find the effort countercultural.

As matters stand, then, neither federal nor state governments have the experience or an incentive to find creative, collaborative solutions to the complex problem of building schools for tomorrow. Local school districts, which do have an incentive, are relatively powerless. Unless something changes, everyone will remain frozen in this unproductive tableau.

The way out is for the partners in the enterprise—federal, state, and local—to redress the imbalance in their relationship. How can each be clear about what it is capable of doing well, about where collaboration is necessary, and about where to cede control? Government has breadth of perspective and broad power. Local educators have special insight into local conditions and the capacity to work deep change at ground level.

A specific example: Both broad policy changes and trench work are needed to improve teaching in a significant way. Governments can require teachers to master core knowledge about content and teaching. They can insist that candidates' work be documented in videos and portfolios. They can set parameters for salaries and benefits and supplement local funding to attract stronger people into the field. They also can supplement funding for staff development networks. At the same time, the actual work of improving teaching has to be local.

WHAT CAN WE DO?

Today's policies have tremendous momentum. The ship won't turn easily or quickly. If it is to take a different course, business leaders will have to conclude that the corporate reform formula does not work well, and that a more balanced approach is in their interest. Elected officials will need to recognize that blaming schools and educators does not improve learning. The public will have to show that they expect and will support something better than what exists. For their part, the media have to do their job: question and examine the issues rigorously.

Critics of corporate reform offer a complicated narrative that, so far, hasn't been either broadly understandable or compelling enough to shift the ground. We need to offer a positive alternative, a clear picture of what education for tomorrow looks like.

The broad outline of that alternative vision is clear. Students engage with challenging content and develop basic skills, but the real goal is to nurture thinkers, problem solvers, human beings. Education is a series of personalized encounters with skilled, caring mentors. Curriculum makes learning meaningful by helping students find connections among ideas and between ideas and experience. Time served in class is less important than whether one can demonstrate depth of understanding. The problem is to ground these principles in practice and to provide concrete examples of what it looks like.

That is a longer-term agenda. In the shorter term, it is important to remember that many Americans already believe a real education is much more than test scores. In Scarsdale, that belief became explicit when parents supported the 2001 test boycott. The community gave the schools latitude to provide children a deep, rich education and let the scores take care of themselves. Essentially, they decided not to let themselves be possessed.

With this history as a backdrop, I met more recently with a group of teachers and administrators to develop a statement on corporate education. The reform movement raises essential questions, they said. "Are we going to educate students or train them?" "Do we want children in the charge of a teacher or a grader?" "Are we talking about helping people grow or about producing an education version of the quarterly report?"

After several weeks, the faculty endorsed a "declaration of intellectual independence." Governments can require schools to give standardized tests and to use them in unsound ways, it said, but nobody can be forced to believe results have a meaning they don't have. The Board of Education and Parent Teacher Council subsequently affirmed the same basic principles. As John Lennon famously said, "You better free your mind" (Lennon & McCartney, 1968).

Other communities also can take control, discount distorted visions of education, and refuse to be victims. In 2012, the school board of the Clear Creek Independent District, located near the Johnson Space Center in Texas, adopted a resolution on the misuses of high-stakes testing in the Lone Star State. More than 400 districts subsequently endorsed a Texas Association of School Administrators position paper on overtesting in a state that was the model for national corporate reform policies (Nix, 2012).

Broad federal and state priorities are unlikely to change immediately. It will take time before America more seriously addresses the challenges of poverty and embraces the complex work of building great schools. But the people who constitute every school district in the United States can endow government policies with whatever significance they choose. We can all make a conscious decision to stop the madness in our own communities now.

Every American also can champion an education that develops human potential, encourages a generous social ethic, and creates a better world. The utilitarian, economic rationale for learning is important. But it is only one reason children go to school. It doesn't necessarily produce curiosity or love of learning, or the innovative spirit that presumably is its own goal. That is a message we can share, and we can tell our elected representatives that we expect something better than corporate reform.

It will be hard to make these points so they will be heard. The corporate ethic is embedded in our culture. It is integral to the way we think. Many people are invested in the notion that it will save public education and that it will make public schools more economical as well. Big money is invested in selling the tests, texts, and technology that are part and parcel of the model. Nonetheless, if the people lead the way, our elected representatives will follow.

WHAT CAN GOVERNMENT DO?

If we are to have world-class schools, the federal government, states, and localities must enter into an authentic partnership, beginning with a willingness to rethink underlying assumptions. The parties each must respect the others' intelligence, competence, and capacities. They must determine which elements of practice are working well now, what might work better, and how to meet today's challenges together.

Nobody has sole claim on the truth. If nothing else, No Child Left Behind should have taught us that sweeping regulation is no more a panacea than the uncoordinated efforts of a decentralized system of localities. To liberate talent instead of reinforcing a lowest common denominator, states have to differentiate responses to objectively different local conditions. Among other things, that means minimizing regulation where it is demonstrably unnecessary and supporting promising local initiative.

Strong teachers and excellent schools can help children overcome huge odds, but a nation that is serious about equalizing educational outcomes and raising the overall level of learning also has to address the effects of poverty, hunger, and unsettled homes. While some existing funding doubtless can be repurposed with this end in mind, the challenge calls for investment that is the equivalent of the Marshall Plan, the 1947 legislation that provided $13 billion to aid in the recovery of a war-ravaged Europe.

The Marshall Plan was expensive. Total gross domestic product in 1948 was $258 billion. Nonetheless, Democrats and Republicans alike had the vision to understand how a failed Europe would threaten the long-term well-being and even the survival of the United States. Public education today is not Europe in the 1940s, but it is a struggling enterprise whose health is essential to America's future.

On reflection, the idea of investing massively in public education may not be so unimaginable. Many in the corporate world understand why children in charter schools need added health, nutrition, and other social services. That's why they provide supplemental funding in the Harlem

Children's Zone, for example. What is missing is the logical leap that would lead them to support added investment in all children from strait-ened circumstances because it is in the public interest. That is one place where the corporate world could exercise meaningful leadership.

The corporate reform strategy is supposed to offer America a better way forward. Instead, it has helped to calcify an outworn industrial-era approach to education that has never been wholly adequate. It has asked relatively little of most of us. The easy course has been to believe in simple solutions and to blame others. Far more difficult would be to each become a voice for reason and to invest ourselves collectively in our common future.

What we want is the imagination and the courage to transform a 2-century-old institution, so that it more fully realizes the promises of democracy. The enterprise calls for an act of will that is unprecedented. Still, if we summon up our strength, we have within us the power to provide America's children the great public education that is still the best hope for tomorrow.

REFERENCES

Adams, K. (2008, December 23). NY's budget mess: Cap spending first. *New York Post*. Retrieved from nypost.com/2008/12/23/nys-budget-mess-cap-spending-first/

Ahlert, A. (2001, April 24). Scarsdale school suckers. *New York Post*, p. 35.

Aten, B., Figueroa, E., & Martin, T. (2012). *Regional price parities for states and metropolitan areas 2006–2010*. Washington, DC: Bureau of Economic Analysis, U.S. Department of Commerce. Retrieved from bea.gov/scb/pdf/2012/08%20August/0812_regional_price_parities.pdf

Berliner, D. C., & Biddle, B. J. (1995). *The manufactured crisis: Myths, fraud and the attack on America's schools*. New York, NY: Addison Wesley.

Berliner, D. C., Glass, G. V., & Associates. (2014). *50 myths and lies that threaten America's public schools*. New York, NY: Teachers College Press.

Berliner, D. C., & Nichols, S. L. (2007). *Collateral damage: How high-stakes testing corrupts America's schools*. Cambridge, MA: Harvard Education Press.

Bestor, A. J. (1985). *Educational wastelands: The retreat from learning in our schools*. Champaign-Urbana: University of Illinois Press. (Original work published 1953)

Blazer, C. (2011). *Unintended consequences of high-stakes testing*. Miami, FL: Miami-Dade County Public Schools. Retrieved from files.eric.ed.gov/fulltext/ED536512.pdf

Bracey, G. W. (2002). *The war on America's public schools*. Boston, MA: Allyn & Bacon.

Bruner, J. (1966). *Toward a theory of instruction*, New York, NY: Norton.

Buffett, W. (2010). *Letter to shareholders*. Retrieved from berkshirehathaway.com/letters/2009ltr.pdf

Bushaw, W. J., & Lopez, S. L. (2013). The 45th Phi Delta Kappa/Gallup poll of the public's attitudes toward the public schools. Bloomington, IN: Phi Delta Kappa. Retrieved from www.pdkintl.org/programs-resources/poll

Business Roundtable. (2001). *Assessing and addressing the "testing backlash": Practical advice and current public opinion research for business coalitions and standards advocates*. Washington, DC: Business Roundtable. Retrieved from eric.ed.gov?id=ED468494

Carmody, D. (1987, March 28). Man in the news; a practical administrator: Dr. Thomas Sobol. *New York Times*. Retrieved from www.nytimes.com/1987/03/25/nyregion/man-in-the-news-a-practical-administrator-dr-thomas-sobol.html

Chilcott, L. (Producer), & Guggenheim, D. (Director). (2010). *Waiting for "Superman."* United States: Walden Media & Participant Media.

Coalition of Essential Schools (CES). (2015). *The CES common principles*. Retrieved from www.essentialschools.org/items/4.html

Coleman, J. S., Campbell, E., Hobson, C., McPartland, J., Mood, A., Weinfeld, F., & York, R. (1966). *Equality of educational opportunity*. Washington, DC: National Center for Education Statistics, Department of Health, Education, and Welfare.

College Board. (2010). *Annual AP program participation 1956–2010*. Retrieved from media.collegeboard.com/digitalServices/pdf/research/AP-Annual-Participation-2010.pdf

Comer, J. P. (2009). *What I learned in school: Reflections on race, child development and school reform*. San Francisco, CA: Jossey Bass.

Cremin, L. (1988). *American education: The metropolitan experience 1876–1980*. New York, NY: Harper & Row.

Cuban, L. (1993). How teachers taught: Consistency and change in American classrooms, 1890–1990 (2nd ed). New York, NY: Teachers College Press.

Cuban, L. (2005). Comments on the paper "Test-based accountability: The promise and the perils," by T. Loveless. Brookings Papers on Education Policy. Washington, DC: Brookings Institution.

Danielson, C. (2007). *Enhancing professional practice: A framework for teaching* (2nd ed.). Alexandria, VA: Association for Supervision and Curriculum Development.

Darling-Hammond, L. (2001, July). Lecture, Teachers College, Columbia University, New York, NY.

Deming, W. E. (1986). *Out of the crisis*. Cambridge, MA: MIT Center for Advanced Engineering.

Dewey, J. (1916). *Democracy and education*. Retrieved from www.gutenberg.org/files/852-h/852-h.htm

Dillon, S. (2004, September 5). Good schools or bad? Ratings baffle parents. *New York Times*. Retrieved from www.nytimes.com/2004/09/05/education/05school.html

Dillon, S. (2011, August 8). Overriding a key education law. *New York Times*. Retrieved from www.nytimes.com/2011/08/08/education/08educ.html

Dobbs, M. (2005, July 15). School achievement gap is narrowing. *Washington Post*. Retrieved from washingtonpost.com/wpdyn/content/article/2005/07/14/AR2005071400718.html

Elmore, R. (2008). *Improving the instructional core*. Retrieved from www.eastbaycharterconnect.org/uploads/7/1/7/6/7176220/improving_the_instructional_core_elmore_2008.pdf

FairTest. (2004). Cheating scandal rocks Texas. Retrieved from www.fairtest.org /Cheating-Scandal-Rocks-Texas

Flesch, R. F. (1955). *Why Johnny can't read: And what you can do about it.* New York, NY: Harper & Row.

Fullan, M. (1982). *The new meaning of educational change.* New York, NY: Teachers College Press.

Fullan, M. (1993). *Change forces: Probing the depths of educational reform.* Levittown, PA: Falmer Press.

Fullan, M. (2001). *Leading in a culture of change.* San Francisco, CA: Jossey-Bass.

Government Accountability Office. (2007) *Reading First: States report improvements in reading instruction but additional procedures would clarify education's role in ensuring proper implementation by states.* Washington, DC: Author. Retrieved from gao.gov/assets/260/257043.html

Gerstner, L., Jr., Semerad, R. D., Doyle, D. P. & Johnston, W. B. (1994). *Reinventing education: Entrepreneurship in America's public schools.* New York, NY: Dutton.

Goldhaber, D. (2002). The mystery of good teaching. *Education Next, 2*(1). Retrieved from educationnext.org/the-mystery-of-good-teaching

Goodman, P. (2001, May 30). Testing the limits. *Newsday.* Retrieved from The newsday.com archive.

Hansen, H. (1954). *Scarsdale: From colonial manor to modern community.* New York, NY: Harper & Brothers.

Harticollis, A. (2001, October 31). No more test boycotts, Scarsdale is warned. *New York Times.* Available at: www.nytimes.com/2001/10/31 /education/31SCAR.html

Heubert, J. P., & Hauser, R. M. (1999). *High stakes: Testing for tracking promotion and grading.* Washington, DC: National Academies Press.

Hout, M., & Elliott, S. W. (Eds.). (2011). *Incentives and test-based accountability in education.* Washington, DC: National Academies Press. Retrieved from www .nap.edu/openbook.php?record_ id=12521

Huffman, K. (2014, August 23). Teaching's human touch. *New York Times.* Retrieved from www.nytimes.com/2014/08/24/opinion/sunday/teachings -human-touch.html

Hutchins, R. M. (1936). *The higher learning in America.* New Haven. CT: Yale University Press.

Hutchins, R. M. (1953). *The university of utopia.* Chicago, IL: University of Chicago Press.

IBM. (2001). *IBM reinventing education: Research summary and perspective.* Retrieved from cct.edc.org/publications/ibm-reinventing-education -summary-and-perspective

Jefferson, T. (1984). Notes on the state of Virginia. In M. D. Peterson (Ed.), *Thomas Jefferson: Writings* (pp. 123ff.). New York, NY: Library of America. (Original work published 1787)

Kohn, A. (2011, April 27). Poor teaching for poor children. *Education Week.* Retrieved from edweek.org/ew/articles/2011/04/27/29kohn.h30html

Koretz, D. (1987). *Educational achievement: Explanations and implications of recent trends*. Washington, DC: Congressional Budget Office. Retrieved from cbo.gov/sites/default/files/doc13b-entire_0.pdf

Koretz, D. M., & Hamilton, L. S. (2003). *Teachers' responses to high-stakes testing and the validity of gains: A pilot study*. Los Angeles, CA: National Center for Research on Evaluation, Standards and Student Testing, UCLA. Retrieved from www.cse.ucla.edu/products/reports/r610.pdf

Lebergott, S. (1960). Wage trends, 1800–1900. In Conference on Research in Income and Wealth (Ed.), *Trends in the American economy in the nineteenth century* (pp. 449–500). Princeton, NJ: Princeton University Press. Retrieved from www.nber.org/chapters/c2486.pdf

Lemann, N. (1999). *The big test*. New York, NY: Farrar, Straus & Giroux.

Lennon, J., & McCartney, P. (1968). Revolution. On *The Beatles* [Record]. London, England: Apple Records.

Lestch, C., & Chapman, B. (2013, March 13). New York parents furious at program, inBloom, that compiles private student information for companies that contract with it to create teaching tools. *New York Daily News*. Retrieved from www.nydailynews.com/new-york/student-data-compiling-system-outrages-article-1.1287990

Leung, R. (2004, January 6). The "Texas miracle." *CBS News*. Retrieved from www.cbsnews.com/news/the-texas-miracle

Mann, H. (1989). *On the art of teaching*. Boston, MA: Applewood Books. (Original work published 1840)

Manzo, K. K. (2005, September 7). States pressed to refashion reading first grant designs; documents suggest federal interference. *Education Week*. Retrieved fromedweek.org/ew/articles/2005/09/07/02read.h25html

Manzo, K. K., & Cavanaugh, S. (2005, July 27). South posts big gains on long-term NAEP in reading and math. *Education Week*. Retrieved from edweek.org/ew/articles/2005/07/27/43naep.h24.html

Marsh, J., Rothstein, R., Figlio, D., & Guthrie, J. (2011, September 20). The debate over teacher merit pay. *Freakonomics*. Retrieved from freakonomics.com/2011/09/20/the-debate-over-teacher-merit-pay-a-freakonomics-quorum/

McCartney, S. (2011). *Child poverty in the United States 2009 and 2010: Selected race groups and Hispanic origin*. Washington, DC: U.S. Bureau of the Census. Retrieved from census.gov/prod2011pubs/acsbr10-05pdf

McGill, M. V. (2001, December 20). Letter to Richard P. Mills, New York State Commissioner of Education.

McIntyre, M. E. (2002). Audit, education and Goodhart's Law: Or, taking rigidity seriously. Retrieved from www.atm.damtp.cam.ac.uk/mcintyre/papers/LHCE/dilnot-analysis.html

Meier, D. (2003, September). The road to trust. *American School Board Journal*. Retrieved from www.asbj.com/MainMenuCategory/Archive/2003/September/The-Road-To-Trust.html

Metcalf, S. (2002, January 28). Reading between the lines. *The Nation*. Retrieved from www.thenation.com/article/reading-between-lines?page=full

Mills, R. P. (2001, October 26). Letter to Michael V. McGill, Superintendent, Scarsdale UFSD.

Mourshad, M., Chijioke, C., & Barber, M. (2010, November). *How the world's most improved school systems keep getting better*. New York, NY: McKinsey & Company. Retrieved from mckinsey.com/client_service/social_sector /latest_thinking/worlds_most_improved_schools

National Center for Education Statistics. (2011). Fast facts. Retrieved from nces .ed.gov/fastfacts/display.asp?id=30

National Center for Education Statistics. (2013). The nation's report card: Trends in academic progress 2012. Retrieved from nces.ed.gov /nationsreportcard

National Commission on Excellence in Education. (1983). *A nation at risk: The imperative for education reform*. Washington, DC: U.S. Government Printing Office.

National Education Association. (2010). *Funding gap: Funding authorized in law vs. funding actually received FY 2002–2011*. Retrieved from nea.org/assets/docs/HE /NCLBFunding.pdf

National Panel on High School and Adolescence. (1974). *Report of the National Panel on High School and Adolescence*. Washington, DC: Department of Health, Education and Welfare.

National Research Council. (2009). *Letter report to the U.S. Department of Education on the Race to the Top Fund*. Washington, DC: Retrieved from nap.edu /openbook.php?record_id=12780&page=2

New York City Department of Education. (2013a). *Progress report 2012-13*. New York, NY: Author. Retrieved from schools.nyc.gov/OA/SchoolReports /2012-13/Progress_Report_2013_HS_Q425.pdf

New York City Department of Education. (2013b). *Chancellor Walcott announces more students are graduating high school ready for college and careers*. New York, NY: Author. Retrieved from schools.nyc.gov/Offices/mediarelations /NewsandSpeeches/2013-2014/CHANCELLOR+WALCOTT+ANNOUNC ES+MORE+STUDENTS+ARE+GRADUATING+HIGH+SCHOOL+READY +FOR+COLLEGE+AND+CAREERS.htm

New York State Education Department. (2003). *School and district accountability reports: Implementing No Child Left Behind (NCLB)*. Albany, NY: Author.

New York State Education Department. (2012). Task-by-task guidance. Albany, NY: Author. Retrieved from www.engageny.org/resource /task-by-task-guidance

New York State Education Department. (2013). *New York State report cards 2012–13*. Albany, NY: Author. Retrieved from data.nysed.gov/enrollment .php?year=2013&instid=800000046798

Nikolski, L. (2001, September 19). Global studies lesson quickly learned. *Journal News*, p. 7B.

Nix, K. (2012, April 30). Flood of Texas school districts staging revolt against high-stakes standardized tests. Retrieved from www.yourhoustonnews.com/pearland/news/flood-of-texas-school-districts-staging-revolt-against-high-stakes/article_379b9b2d-9a5d-503a-b186-aa37bd35b4aa.html

Obama, B. (2011). *State of the Union address*. Retrieved from whitehouse.gov/the-press-office/2011/01/25/remarks-president-state-union-address

Ohanian, S. (2006). Commentaries: High standards. Retrieved from www.susanohanian.org/show_commentaries.php?id=571

Parks, S. (2005, March 6) The big man on campus reform. *Dallas Morning News*. Retrieved from: texasedequity.blogspot.com/2005/03/big-man-on-campus-reform.html

Pear, R. (2004, February 24). Education chief calls union "terrorist" then recants. *New York Times*. Retrieved from www.nytimes.com/2004/02/24/us/education-chief-calls-union-terrorist-then-recants.html

Pearson. (2014). Pearson 2013 results. Retrieved from www.pearson.com/news/announcements/2014/february/pearson-2013-results.html

Popham, J. (2004). *America's "failing" schools*. New York, NY: Routledge Falmer.

Rampell, C. (2009, November 24). Tax burdens, around the world. *New York Times*. Retrieved economix.blogs.nytimes.com/2009/11/24/the-tax-burden-around-the-developed-world/

Ravitch, D. (1983). *The troubled crusade: American education 1945–1980*. New York, NY: Basic Books.

Ravitch, D. (2010). *The death and life of the great American school system: How testing and choice are undermining education*. New York, NY: Basic Books.

Ravitch, D. (2013). *Reign of error: The hoax of the privatization movement and the danger to America's public schools*. New York, NY: Knopf.

Ravitch, D., & Elmore, R. (2002). *Brookings papers on educational policy 2002*. Washington, DC: Brookings Institution.

Ritchie, C. C. (1972, February). The eight year study: Can we afford to ignore it? *Educational Leadership*. Retrieved from www.ascd.org/ASCD/pdf/journals/ed_lead/el_197102_ritchie.pdf

Rose, L. C., & Gallup, A. M. (2004). The 36th annual Phi Delta Kappa/Gallup poll of the public's attitudes toward the public schools. *Phi Delta Kappan*. Bloomington, IN: Phi Delta Kappa.

Rosenthal, R., & Jacobson, L. (1968). *Pygmalion in the classroom: Teacher expectations and pupils' intellectual development*. New York, NY: Rinehart and Winston.

Rothschild, A. (1977). *It didn't just happen: The story of the Scarsdale schools*. Unpublished, Scarsdale, NY.

Rothstein, R. (1998). *The way we were? Myths and realities of America's student achievement*. New York, NY: Century Foundation.

Rothstein, R. (2008). *Grading education: Getting teacher accountability right*. New York, NY: Teachers College Press.

Saphier, J., Speca, M-A. H., & Gower, R. (2008). *The skillful teacher: Building your teaching skills.* Concord, MA: Research for Better Teaching.

Sarason, S. (1990). *The predictable failure of educational reform.* San Francisco, CA: Jossey-Bass.

Schemo, D. J. (2003, April 10). Church–state furor engulfs education chief. *New York Times.* Retrieved from www.nytimes.com/2003/04/10/US /church-state-furor-engulfs-education-chief.html

Schmitt, J., Warner, K., & Gupta, S. (2010). *The high budgetary cost of incarceration.* Washington, DC: Center for Economic and Policy Research. Retrieved from www.cepr.net/documents/publications/incarceration-2010-06.pdf

Silberman, C. E. (1970). *Crisis in the classroom.* New York, NY: Random House.

Snyder, T. D. (1993). *120 years of American education: A statistical portrait.* Washington, DC: National Center for Education Statistics. Retrieved from nces.ed.gov/pubs93/93442.pdf

Strauss, V. (2011, Dec. 7). Do teachers really come from the 'bottom third' of college graduates? *Washington Post.* Retrieved from www.washingtonpost .com/blogs/answer-sheet/post/do-teachers-really-come-from-the -bottom-third-of-college-graduates/2011/12/07/gIQAg8HPdO_blog.html

Tri-State Consortium. (2010). Report of the tri-state visiting committee. Scarsdale, NY.

Urban Academy. (2013). *Urban Academy.* New York, NY. Retrieved from urbanacademy.org/alternative/alternative.html

U.S. Bureau of the Census. (2010). *Public education finances 2008.* Retrieved from www2.census.gov/govs/school/08f33pub.pdf

U.S. Department of Education. (2009). Race to the Top program executive summary. Washington, DC: Author. Retrieved from www2.ed.gov/programs /racetothetop/executive-summary.pdf

U.S. Department of Education, Office of the Inspector General. (2006). *The Reading First program's grant application process. Final inspection report* (ED-OIG/113 -F0017). Washington, DC: U.S. Department of Education. Retrieved from www2.ed.gov/about/offices/list/oig/aireports/i13f0017.pdf

Winters, R. (2001, February 12). Teacher in chief. *Time.* Retrieved from content.time.com/time/magazine/article/0,9171,999206,00.html

Zernicke, K. (2001, April 13). In high-scoring Scarsdale, a revolt against state tests. *New York Times.* Retrieved from www.nytimes.com/2001/04/13 /nyregion/in-high-scoring-scarsdale-a-revolt-against-state-tests.html

INDEX

ABOUT THE AUTHOR

Michael V. McGill, EdD, is director of the Program for District Leadership and Reform at the Bank Street Graduate School of Education in New York City.

He was superintendent of the Scarsdale, NY, public schools from 1998 to 2014. In 2007, the New York State Council of School Superintendents named him Superintendent of the Year, based on his "outstanding all-around leadership."

He began his career as superintendent in 1973 in the Mt. Greylock District in Williamstown, MA. He also served as headmaster of the Hopkins School in New Haven, CT, and as superintendent of the North Shore Schools in Sea Cliff, NY.

McGill graduated from Williams College and received a master's degree in teaching and a doctorate in education from Harvard University. He and his wife, Pucci, live in a 260-year-old home in northwest Connecticut.